BAGHDAD-BY-THE-BAY

an odd name for a column about a city . . .

It is an even odder thing to consider here in the Eighties that the name Baghdad once carried the connotation of an imagined place, a crossroads of strange and exotic people and the things they created. It was more a place in the mind than it was a place on the map, or worse, on the front pages of the newspaper that carries his column, *The San Francisco Chronicle*.

But that is what the column was called when this book was first published, and when Harry Truman was in the White House and Ronald Reagan was still in Hollywood. It is useful to read this book today because it tells us not just names and dates and events and places . . . it presents a glimpse at the fabric of the City at a time of great hope and great confidence. Perhaps BAGHDAD BY THE BAY can leave us with an insight into what the charm of this imagined place is all about. If you are lucky enough to know (or can find) some people who were here then and knew what the City was like, then maybe they will explain some of the names and places for you . . . they might even throw in some tidbits about the Crystal Palace Market and Sutro Baths and a few other things that are gone now . . . Be respectful of this heritage and you may one day approach native status and start calling it The City and find it very easy to think back to the times when it might have been a magical place called *Baghdad By The Bay*.

BAGHDAD-BY-THE-BAY

Herb Caen

A COMSTOCK EDITION

The author gratefully acknowledges the *San Francisco Chronicle* for
permission to reprint material previously
published in its pages.

This edition published by arrangement with
Doubleday & Co., Inc.

Additional copies of this book may be obtained by sending a check or money
order for the price of the book plus one dollar for the first copy and seventy-
five cents for each additional copy. A free catalog of books published by
Comstock is available by mail from this address:

COMSTOCK EDITIONS, INC.
3030 Bridgeway, Sausalito, CA 9496

CHAPTERS

CONTENTS

1.

BAGHDAD-BY-THE-BAY

San Francisco, to me, is like a house of cards: post cards in glowing colors stacked against the hills that march from the Bay on one side to the Pacific Ocean on the other.

The real magic of the city lies in the way these snapshots remain in the mind, no one impressed more sharply on the consciousness than the next. And when I am far away, the city's myriad details come floating back to me as though they were unwinding endlessly on the movie screen of my memory.

Each picture is sharp and complete, glamorized a little by a wisp of fog in one corner and a pennant streaming in the wind atop a skyscraper. It's a sentimental, perhaps corny, way to look at a city, but the San Franciscan is hopelessly sentimental, and I am hopelessly San Franciscan.

To me, my city is Baghdad-by-the-Bay, and my mind is

1

lined—yes, even cluttered—with its pictures, ranged side by side. Like this:

By the dawn's early light Coit Tower standing starkly silhouetted against the first faint flush in the east . . . A sun-and-windswept corner on Montgomery Street, where you can look west and see a wall of thick, dirty fog rising genii-like from the Pacific, while a finger of whiter, puffier stuff feels its way into the Bay, twisting this way and that till it conforms to every contour, snugly and coldly . . . And the poor man's perfume of Skid Road—a melancholy mixture of frying grease, stale beer, and harsh deodorants that clings to your clothes and your thoughts for hours.

The smug majesty of the City Hall's famed dome, higher (and dirtier) than Washington's, and so far above the conniving that goes on beneath it . . . The few surviving little wooden houses of Telegraph Hill, clinging together for mutual protection against concrete newcomers slowly pushing them out on a limbo . . . And Fisherman's Wharf at 7 A.M., with its tiny fleet of tiny ships lined up in neat display, and proud sea gulls strutting past to review them.

The aged hangers-on outside the Public Library in Civic Center, singing an *a cappella* chorus of futility against the roaring backdrop of a metropolis in motion—Market Street . . . That occasional white ferryboat drifting over from the Oakland mole and dipping respectfully beneath the aloof bridge that doomed so many of its side-wheeling sisters . . . And block after block of flatiron buildings along Columbus

2

Avenue—sharp edges of a city that grew in too many directions at once.

The incongruity of a lonely foghorn calling somewhere in the Bay as you stroll hatless down a sun-swept street—and the grotesque sight of this jumbled city from Twin Peaks, a sardonic, hysterical travesty on the dreams of those who stood there after the Great Fire and planned the Perfect City . . . Long-forgotten cable-car slots wandering disconsolately and alone up steep hills that are now flattened, with a contemptuous snort, by high-powered, twin-engined busses . . . And the Saturday-night symphony audiences arriving breathlessly at the Opera House from streetcars, on foot, in shabby automobiles—a far and enjoyable cry from the Friday-afternoon trade slinking slowly up in limousines that actually look bored.

University of California's Medical Center (where they discovered vitamin E) rearing up like a spectacular movie set against the darkness of Mount Sutro and Parnassus Heights, while in the pre-dawn hush of Golden Gate Park, far below, squirrels sit unafraid in the middle of the silent roads, and ducks waddle importantly along the bridle paths . . . The full magnificence of the Pacific bursting into your consciousness as you swing past the Cliff House . . . And the monumental mechanical madness of the Kearny, Geary, Third, and Market intersection, where traffic, honking the horns of its dilemma, squeezes painfully through a bottleneck with a "Stop" sign for a cork.

The too-bright mask of Chinatown's restaurants and bars,

sometimes standing half empty, while upstairs, in the tene-
mentlike apartments, live six Chinese in one room . . . The
glittering Golden Horseshoe during opera season, a constant
reminder that there are Upper Classes even in a public building paid for by the masses . . . And the eye-bulging sight,
from atop the Fifteenth Avenue hill, of the little white new
houses marching through the Sunset District toward the
Pacific like stucco lemmings that decided, just in time, not
to hurl themselves into the sea.

St. Francis Wood, Pacific Heights, and Sea Cliff, where
the homes have room to puff out their chests in the satisfaction of success; and the ornate frame buildings just west of
Van Ness—before 1906 the mansions of the mighty, today
living out their long lives as boardinghouses for those who
are also merely existing . . . Those two distinguished neighbors, the Mark Hopkins and the Fairmont, staring blankly
at each other across California Street in the silence of
5 A.M., when even the cable slots cease their friendly gib-
berish . . . And the corner of Jackson and Kearny, a one-
worldly blend of China, Italy, and Mexico, where, all within
a few steps, you can eat chow mein, top it off with chianti,
and then step into a Spanish movie.

The inner excitement of Stockton Tunnel, as the jam-
packed F cars wiggle noisily through, autos somehow squeeze
past, and school kids run excitedly along the inside walk;
and North Beach, with its 1001 neon-splattered joints alive
with the Italian air of garlic and the juke-boxed wail of
American Folk songs . . . The dismal reaches of lower

4

BAGHDAD-BY-THE-BAY

Market after midnight; the city within a city that is the deep Mission District, and the bittersweet juxtaposition of brusquely modern Aquatic Park against the fortresslike jumble of red brick where Ghiradelli makes his chocolate.

The crowded garages and the empty old buildings above them, the half-filled night clubs and the overfilled apartment houses, the saloons in the skies and the families huddled in basements, the Third Street panhandlers begging for hand-outs in front of pawnshops filled with treasured trinkets, the great bridges and the rattletrap streetcars, the traffic that keeps moving although it has no place to go, the thousands of newcomers glorying in the sights and sounds of a city they've suddenly decided to love, instead of leave . . .

This is Baghdad-by-the-Bay!

2.

THE LITTLE THINGS THAT COUNT

San Francisco. Sentimental expatriates say, "You can leave it—but it never leaves you." It has three approaches by land, only one of which is free. It is full of fleas that bite only tourists and newcomers, never natives. It is against the law to bet on horse races, but there are three tracks in neighboring counties and the radio stations announce the results as soon as they are received and the newspapers build circulation by giving free trips to Santa Anita. And the sailors of the Pacific Fleet call it "Bar Harbor."

San Francisco. Chinatown delights the visitors and sickens the Health Department because its tuberculosis rate is the highest in town. Baseball Hero Lefty O'Doul has no connection with a saloon called "Left O'Doul's," and Baseball Hero Joe DiMaggio has no connection with a Fisherman's Wharf restaurant called "DiMaggio's." Market Street is not only the

6

noisiest Main Street in the country, among big cities, but also the shortest. And Maiden Lane, the "cutest" midtown street, was once the heart of the red-light district.

San Francisco. State Assemblyman Thomas Maloney, the son of a rugged South o' the Slot saloonkeeper, has never had a drink in his life. The Marx Brothers run a string of cigar stores, Carl Marx is a bartender, the Warner Brothers are in the corset business, and there is no liaison, financial or otherwise, between the Love Brassière Shop on Grant Avenue and the Love Investment Company on Post Street. And a favorite drink along Skid Road is milk mixed with gasoline.

San Francisco. The America-Mexico Company operates a Chinese grocery. The Fife Building on Drumm Street wasn't so named in a fit of whimsey, but only because its original owner was a Mr. Fife. On April Fool's Day, for years, the busiest man in town was a Mr. Seal, who worked at the Steinhart Aquarium. The White House and the City of Paris are department stores, and the Forbidden City is a night club, and the City of Hankow manufactures tassels. And there's a downtown fur store called Fur Manchu.

San Francisco. There is a Los Angeles Hotel on California Street, but no San Francisco Hotel—unless you count the San Fran Hotel in Chinatown. George Washington is an engineer, and "Awful Fresh" MacFarlane, who makes candy, is more bashful than "Bashful" Smith, who makes blueprints for a living. And "Shorty" Roberts, who runs an atmospheric restaurant at the Beach, is renowned as the man who once swam across the Golden Gate while hanging onto a horse named "Blackie."

San Francisco. The Top o' the Mark, a drinking place atop the Mark Hopkins Hotel, grosses more than $1,500,000 a year, and Blum's, a tiny corner candy store, grosses $3,000,-000. The Fox Theater modestly describes itself as the "World's Finest," and a place called Hellwig's offers "The World's Best Chicken Pies," and the Union Square Garage is the "World's Finest Underground Garage," and a Van Ness Avenue restaurant called the "Chicken House" features roast beef. "In a Pinch, Call Lynch," advertises a bail bond broker named Frank Lynch, who adds, "If You're Bailable, We're Available."

San Francisco. Good neighbors on Bush Street, between Powell and Mason, are O'Sullivan's liquor store, Myers' tailor shop, Gaddini's cocktail lounge, and Leland Yee's Chinese Laundry. The Messrs. Illa Millnovich, N. Katurich, A. Kovacevich, and M. Zambelich owned a famous old Montgomery Street café called Collins & Wheeland. Daniel B. Seeds runs a nursery on Clement Street, C. G. Branch is an executive with the California Nursery Company, and the officer in charge of Marine Corps recruiting is a Major Gunner whose daughter is named Maureen Gunner. Made in San Francisco: Hollywood Diet Reducing Bread.

San Francisco. In Janet Barry's beauty parlor for dogs a warming slug of brandy and milk is available for the more delicate animals, so they won't catch cold after their shampoos. William F. Humphrey, president of the Associated Oil

Company, has offices in the Standard Oil Building; he has been elected president of a leading men's organization, the Olympic Club, every year since 1907. The sign over a bare and dirty table in a corner of an Embarcadero restaurant reads: "This Table Reserved for Drunks." And the William Tell House, a polka-and-schottische rendezvous on Clay Street, has two signs which indicate the diversity of its clientele: "Liverwurst Sandwiches, 15 Cents," and "Champagne, $2.50."

San Francisco. The best residential sections get most of the fog, and the poorest district gets most of the sunshine. Electric fly killers adorn the cages at Fleishhacker Zoo, so the animals won't have to bother. Treasure Island, the man-made navy base in the middle of the Bay, isn't really an island at all, because it's connected to Yerba Buena Island. In the Mission District there's a "Skyscraper Café" one story high. The Wells Fargo Bank isn't in the Wells Fargo Building; it's in the Nevada Bank Building on Montgomery Street. The Wells Fargo Building is occupied by the telephone company.

San Francisco. A dentist named Dr. Beauchamp spends thousands of dollars advertising that his name is pronounced "Beecham." The horns on the Dy-dee Wash baby laundry trucks sound out the four notes of "Rock-a-bye Baby." A favorite, ageless gag of the newsboys is to shout: "Extry, extry —big accident! Market Street runs into the Ferry!" A. Boxer runs a beauty parlor, Benjamin Franklin is a printer, and Rip Van Winkle is manager of a "Wide-Awake Sales & Service" Company. And there are no seals on world-famous Seal Rocks; only sea lions.

San Francisco. You can eat on Geary Street at the Eatwell (if you're a gourmet) or directly across the street at the Eatmore (if you're a gourmand). On the same street, a few blocks away, you can shop at the Safeway, the E-Z Way, or the Cashway markets. You can have your hair cut by the Barber of Seville, your shoes shined by King Jazz, and your nails manicured by a Miss Nail, who recently married a Mr. Emery. If you're hungry, you can eat at the Fly Trap, the Dump, the Ground Cow, the Old Crab House, the Pig Pen, the Alley, and the Sawdust Inn. And if your sex is right, you can have your hair done in a beauty parlor on Geary near Larkin that advertises petulantly: "This beauty parlor is for women only."

San Francisco. A thirteen-year-old girl named Dolly Fritz owns the fashionable Huntington Hotel on Nob Hill; her father gave it to her. Joe Parente, a fabulous figure in the bootlegging era (he was so big "Baby-Face" Nelson was merely one of his employees), owns a small corner saloon in North Beach. The real name of the engineer who runs the miniature steam train at Fleishhacker Zoo is Casey Jones. One John Quigley not only lives in a penthouse atop the Drake-Wiltshire Hotel—the penthouse has a barbecue pit. And, for sentimental reasons, the bronze corner plaque outside the City of Paris department store still lists Gaston Verdier as president of the firm, although he has been dead since 1915.

San Francisco. The slogan of the Scavengers' Association (the garbage collectors) is "Always at Your Disposal"—and one of its members advertises: "It may be garbage to you, but it's bread and butter to me!" George Swett is in the ventilating business, Mr. Schade sells Venetian blinds, I. Dye is an insurance adjuster with Royal Indemnity, and Edith Klock is a secretary in the main office of the Time Oil Company. The five Hand brothers—Delbert, Frank, Harold, Lee, and Mark—are all doctors with offices in the 450 Sutter Building, specializing in almost everything except hands.

San Francisco. The biggest American Legion Post in town is the Cathay—100 per cent Chinese. According to the sign on his plant in the Mission District, "C. W. Marwedel Taps and Dies." The Precisely Liquor Store is in the Fillmore District, and on Stockton Street is located the Splendid Candy Company, which apparently doesn't make splendid candy at all; the sign on its window says simply "Fine Candy." The general manager of Radio Station KSAN is Lee Mikesell. Among the employees of a South San Francisco packing house are the Messrs. White, Gray, Blue, Brown, and Green, all of whom are Negro—and a Mr. Black, who is white.

San Francisco. The Market Hotel isn't on Market Street, but on Washington. The offices of the Market Street Railway are on Sutter Street. The Market Street Van & Storage Company is on Mission Street. And the Masonic Temple isn't on Masonic Avenue, but on Van Ness. There's a Los Angeles Avenue and a Hollywood Court, but no street named San Francisco. The Italian-American Society Hall is on Russia Avenue, near London Street—and Naples and Italy streets are in the Mission, miles from the Italian section. And the San Francisco Yacht Club, second oldest in the United States, isn't in San Francisco, but across the Bay in Belvedere.

San Francisco. You can get your shoes polished at the Sit'n'Chat Shoe Shine Shop on First Street, drop in for a snack at the Chew'n'Chat restaurant in the Fillmore sector, and get your hair done at the Cut'n'Kurl Beauty Shop on Mission. A liquor store on Market, near First, invites passersby to "Come in and Booze Around Awhile." Alexis, David, Robert, Fred, and Ida Benioff, all related, are in the fur business at separate establishments within a block of one another. On Turk near Taylor stands the Argue Hotel ("Don't Argue—Stay at the Argue") which was merely the maiden name of the woman who once owned it. A restaurant on Ellis near Steiner, featuring "Home-cooked Food," calls itself the Wee Wee Café. And the telephone girls at the Carnation Milk Company greet incoming calls with "Moo to you!"

San Francisco. The cost of living has gone up to the point where it now costs $45 instead of $30 to file for bankruptcy. There are more federal employees than in any other city outside of Washington, D.C.; more telephones per capita than in any other city in the country, including Washington, D.C.; and more drunks arrested per capita than in any other big city in the country, especially including New York City, which is last on the list. The second longest non-transfer railroad trip in the world is from the Third and Townsend Station to Guatemala—4000 miles on one ticket (longest is the trans-Siberian run). Insurance companies still take a chance on the Cliff House—although every previous Cliff House in history burned down. And more swimming champions have been produced here than anywhere else in the country, although swimmers are advised to stay out of the ocean because it's too dangerous, and hardly anybody swims at the biggest outdoor salt-water swimming pool in the world (Fleishhacker) because it's too cold.

San Francisco. Its official motto is *Oro en paz, fierro en guerra*—"Gold in peace, iron in war." William Howard Taft contributed its most famous slogan when he called it "The city that knows how," to which disgruntled present-day citizens add: "But when?" Countless other notables have lavished their praise on Baghdad-by-the-Bay, but it remained for a visiting Chicagoan named Keith Wheeler to contribute a line that, in the two years since he first uttered it, has already become a classic: "East is East, but West is—San Francisco!"

3.

THIS IS SAN FRANCISCO

The vagrant perfume from a sidewalk flower stand that you pass every day but seldom patronize . . . The tall ladies and the dumpy ones, the fat ladies and the thin ones, staring raptly into the handsome showwindows at I. Magnin's—merely to see their own reflections . . . The no-parking signs, the red zones, the white zones, the yellow zones, the green zones, the white lines, the purple-faced cops, the signals, the horns, the waving of many arms—and the safety-zone buttons that cut your tires and provide safety for no one . . . The shiny new store fronts in Chinatown, the brand-new headquarters of a "Family Association" on Waverly Place, the Chinese restaurants that serve you more food than you can possibly eat—and the sallow-faced children sandwiched into tenements where only disease has enough room to flourish.

The new addition to Macy's and the new addition to Standard Oil and the new addition to PG&E and the new white houses blossoming in the sand—and the earnest young veterans without jobs, walking the streets in their endless search for the homes they fought for, at a price they can pay . . . The last rusty old streetcar rattling around the loop in front of the dusty, musty, ghostlike Ferry Building—old friends that have a lot to talk about, nothing to live for, and nobody to care any more . . . The little businessmen complaining that the wet weather keeps the customers away, the night-club owners wringing their hands over empty tables, idle moviehouse cashiers manicuring their nails—and 19,000 standing in the rain at Golden Gate Fields.

The panorama from Lafayette Park, sweeping across the stately, sugar-frosty Spreckels mansion and the middle-class Marina to Alcatraz, San Francisco's Château D'Ifficult . . . Tennis players in spotless white ducks batting a white tennis ball back and forth in the California Tennis Club, under the earnest gaze of Negro children watching from their dingy wooden houses on the other side of the fence, on the other side of the street . . . School children bouncing busily up the front stairs of the Public Library, while right around the corner the tired old men sit along the wall in a deep frieze and think about the lessons that they've learned—too late . . . The pigeons in Union Square, scuttling just ahead of your footsteps like kids enjoying an expressionless, soundless game of tag.

The Reillys and the O'Days and the Moskovitzes and the Cunninghams and the Figones in the St. Patrick's Day Parade, full of good brotherhood and the spirit of the day that brought De Valera to Market Street and the Freedom Train to the Marina—two symbols that came a long way to remind us that we have a long way to go . . . The cats that prowl the by-ways of the produce district, growing sleek on the scraps that are thrown away—and the gaunt wraiths that prowl the alleys of Skid Road, peering into garbage cans with eyes that no longer hope . . . The bareheaded tenderloin types, standing in knots of twos and threes on the Taylor street corners with their speech full of four-letter words, their gaze as slouchy as their stance, their hands in pockets that are as empty as their ambition.

The young men of Montgomery Street, recently out of uniforms they dread getting back into, marching energetically through the financial marts in their all-alike attire of gray sack suits, black knit ties, and white button-down shirts—from olive drab to just plain drab . . . International Settlement's one brittle block, filled with drunks and socialites and ex-cons and good entertainers and lousy entertainers and cops and stool pigeons—everything, in fact, but public dancing, because this is indecent and might lead to a return of the Barbary Coast, says the law . . . The crest of Nob Hill, where Huntington Park prohibits dogs, the Pacific-Union Club prohibits more than dogs, and in a fabulously valuable vacant lot the wind toys with old scraps of paper and rats scurry through empty fruit boxes . . . Serious-faced policemen putt-puttering along the streets on their tricycles to make chalk marks on the tires of parked cars—the dignity of the law reduced to the kid-on-a-scooter level.

THIS IS SAN FRANCISCO

Newly formed whitish fog filtering through the harp strings of the Golden Gate Bridge and then puffing out its chest as though pleased with its dramatic entrance; but the only applause is the quiet lapping of the waves as they disappear under the silent mass . . . The deserted midtown streets after midnight, punctuated by the sound of a window closing suddenly, the sharp click of an apartment-house door, a radio playing softly down the hall, the rattle of cabs taking girls from their own hotel to somebody else's . . . The Sunday golfers hard at play on the broad green acres in Lincoln Park and the Presidio and Harding Park and Lakeside, while the kids of North Beach tumble down the hills on homemade gadgets and the kids of Chinatown play handball against a saloon wall and the kids of the Mission shinny up telephone poles and get calluses on their hearts.

The cable-car conductors running to the rear platform to signal a sudden turn, the cabbies stopping suddenly with no signal whatever, the tiny old houses with the million-dollar views, the financial district skyscrapers whose denizens are too busy to look out the windows, the restaurants where you may "eat around the world," and the old people who have come around the world to find something to eat . . . All this, and so much more, is San Francisco.

4.

ALL THROUGH THE DAY

Let's see how a day looks in San Francisco.

To those who bend over a desk or a hot stove for eight hours, I guess a day in San Francisco is pretty much like a day in Des Moines or Birmingham. But if you have a chance to spend those daylight hours just looking around, you run across those little "different" touches that give the typical San Francisco day its own flavor.

At dawn the Bay looks as corny and unreal as a penny post card. The sky behind the Oakland hills starts to flush and grow streaky with light, and the somber waters slowly become luminous. Gradually the markers of the night go out—the swinging beacons atop the Bridge towers, the dramatic light on Alcatraz, the Drake's evening star, and the Mark's blue topper. There is a final, breathless moment, as though the sun were trying to decide whether to catch a little more sleep, and then suddenly the shadows call it a night and pull the covers over their heads. A damp, scrubbed freshness comes into the air and the invisible hand of a new day sets off a thousand alarm clocks and begins to rub its sleepy eyes.

For a youngster just out of night clothes, Today makes a lot of noise. The garbage trucks, nearing the end of their run, raise a self-conscious commotion, as though to drown out the doubtful perfume they leave in the air. In the produce district, alive and on the job for hours, the tempo is quickened, for the work is almost done. Motormen clang a little more authoritatively as traffic comes to life, and the little men who live inside the traffic signals awaken and pull back their shutters. Along Skid Road the panhandlers shift uncomfortably in the doorways they use for bedrooms and wish they had a shade to pull down.

Only the birds greet Today with brightness and chirps of pleasure. The tired lovebirds who necked and parked too long at Coit Tower look up sullenly as the sun begins to arch over the Bridge and then glance around self-consciously as he grinds on the starter and she tries to smooth her wrinkled feathers. The early commuters stomp through Third and Townsend and pack themselves into streetcars, some grumbling already, others staring dully at newspapers, a few trying unsuccessfully to catch a catnap on the rear platform. In the waffle shops along Powell and on Turk the stubble-faced night owls gulp down black coffee and shudder slightly as the freshly shaved denizens of the day dash in for ham and

19

eggs. Only Golden Gate Park seems to awaken gracefully and begins to shake the sequins of the night off its green shoulders.

The new day starts to develop wrinkles at an early age. The trucks begin their routine of double-parking, and soon there is a traffic snarl with cops to match. The small shopkeepers, already gray around the gills, open their front doors, switch off the little neon sign, and then stand outside for a few minutes, sniffing the air and wondering idly where the first customer will come from and why. Along Eddy and Ellis the day clerks in the tiny hotels yawn and go about their daily routine of shaking the servicemen who slept all night in the lobby. The stenos of Montgomery Street, most of whom snoozed five minutes too long again, dash madly into office buildings, their fine legs twinkling competition for the inexorable hands on the clock.

Out in the neighborhoods, where life is as monotonous as the houses it whithers away in, Today brings a certain excitement. At each door the same never-ending little drama is enacted. Each backbone of the community flies through the front door, his overcoat tails flapping, and each little woman stands there in her wrapper to watch the lord and master clatter away. He waits at the corner, makes the usual comment about the streetcar service, exchanges a remark about the weather —and reflects bitterly that back in their almost-paid-for home his wife is settling down for another cup of coffee and "Dick Tracy." That night he will come home to recount his hard day at the office, and she will tell of her hard day shopping, and both will feel sorry for themselves, but not for each other.

ALL THROUGH THE DAY

The sun has pulled itself higher now, and the shadows are gone from the downtown canyons. The big executives arrive at their skyscrapers, reasonably late, to bump into their red-faced junior execs en route to the midmorning cup of java. Already the early shoppers are complaining about their feet and high prices, and pretty soon the fancier ladies who have spent the morning at their dressing tables will filter into El Prado and the smart hotels to plunge forks into salads and knives into backs. The businessmen who try to make a splash by taking clients to the Palace discover they have no appointments and sidle alone into the cheaper sandwich shops. The morning newspapers disappear from the corner stands and the afternoons, having rewritten the headlines slightly, pop up in their places. The line of cars outside Union Square Garage grows longer, matching the faces of the drivers.

The day becomes mellow and easier to get along with as it ages. The whole town seems to relax; the fog creeps in and the sun, not so young as it used to be, loses its grip on the heavens. The office girls duck into drugstores for a late-afternoon Coke, and the guys, realizing they're over the hump, stick in the cigar store for another pinball game and make cynical cracks as they watch the boss hustle away to the Olympic Club. In the cocktail salons the bartenders consult their watches and begin dropping olives into martini glasses, a slice of orange and a cherry into the old-fashioned holders. The lone dolls on the high stools hurriedly apply a new coat of lipstick and start staring at the door. Then five o'clock strikes with a crash heard throughout the city, the streetcars brace themselves for

21

the rush, the cops take a firmer grip on their whistles—and so to bedlam. And meanwhile, out beyond the lonely Farallones the sun that started all this sinks without a sizzle into the Pacific, painting the sky with a farewell burst of glory. Weakly the street lamps take over the job, and day is done.

5.

THE BIG NAMES

For a world-famous city, San Francisco has a surprisingly small coterie of so-called "celebrities" (a celebrity being, I would say, someone who is widely known outside his own community and his own field of endeavor). There are dozens of purely local celebrities, shaking hands and being pointed out every time they walk down the street, but as for the large, economy-size celebrity, as likely to pop up in Winchell's column as my own, I can think of only a handful—for example, Lefty O'Doul, Harry Bridges, William Saroyan, Kathleen Norris, Joe DiMaggio, Pierre Monteux.

There are more, of course, but these are the first that come to mind, perhaps because they pass the sternest test for qualification as celebrities. Their names need no appositional identification. You know by this time that Kathleen Norris is a writer, whether you've read her stuff or not. Harry Bridges can be described as "well-known" or "widely known," depending on your point of view. And if there's a better symphony conductor in the world than Pierre Monteux, San Franciscans would rather not hear about him.

On the fringe of this select circle is a group of satellite celebrities. I'm not quite sure whether the citizens of Oshkosh or Peoria ever heard of Roger Dearborn Lapham, but stories about him fill envelopes in newspaper "morgues" all over the country. Shipowner, mayor, administrator of economic aid to China, "Roger Dodger" Lapham has made his mark.

He is especially celebrated along the water front as the first employer willing to trade verbiage on a public debating platform with Harry Bridges, a notoriously quick thinker on his feet. The historic encounter took place before a mob of 10,000 in Civic Auditorium in the mid-thirties, and Roger gave a good account of himself, even drawing a cheer now and then from the antagonistic longshoremen.

It was around this time that an automobile accident of more than passing interest took place at Howard and Beale streets, near the Embarcadero. A sleek sedan traded blows with a truck, then turned over and came to a precarious halt on its top. A crowd collected (yes, as if by magic). A couple of longshoremen yanked open the doors of the sedan and pulled out the driver, a gray-haired portly gentleman still smoking his cigar. He and it were uninjured.

"Say," said one of the rescuing longshoremen, "you're Roger Lapham, aren't you?" Lapham nodded.

"Well," snapped the water fronter, "I saw the accident, pal. And for the first time in your life—you're right!"

THE BIG NAMES

Another "fringe" celebrity is Herbert Fleishhacker, whose name might mean nothing to you, but is, nevertheless, permanently engraved on several San Francisco institutions.

In 1930, when he was perhaps the West's most prominent banking figure, Herbert happened to be strolling through the Himalayas in India with an old friend named Louis D. Stone. Suddenly Fleishhacker sniffed the air and said: "Lou, I smell animals around here somewhere." They investigated and discovered some caged tigers and lions, newly caught by a trapper. "I'll buy them," declared Fleishhacker with the simple grandiloquence of the successful banker—and thus, then and there, was born Fleishhacker Zoo, today one of San Francisco's proudest landmarks.

(Possibly apocryphal footnote: On a Sunday afternoon at Fleishhacker Zoo a small child was heard crying: "Mommy, I'm tired of looking at monkeys and elephants. Where are the fleishhackers?")

San Francisco's favorite "Horatio Alger" personality is Louis R. Lurie, who, for want of a more exact title, is known as a tycoon. Once a newsboy in his native Chicago, Lurie today is one of the nation's cagiest real estate operators, a collector of new and used skyscrapers from coast to coast, a heavyweight dabbler in theatrical enterprises, and a dogged host to the great and near-great.

For more than thirty years he has lunched at the same table in a corner of Jack's Rotisserie, an excellent French restaurant on Sacramento Street in the financial district. At this table, where Louis is always host, you're likely to find yourself sitting between Noel Coward and Gertrude Lawrence—or, on a less celebrated day, between Mouthpiece J. W. "Jake" Ehrlich and Politico "Honest George" Reilly. Others who feed their faces there regularly include Parker Maddux, president of the San Francisco Bank; Mayor James Howell of Atherton; Comedian Lou Holtz, and occasional underfed, underpaid newspaper columnists. (Note to the Collector of Internal Revenue: I always insist on paying my share. Of the tip.)

As befits a man who has risen high in the world, Lurie is addicted to high places. His offices are in the eighteenth-floor penthouse of 333 Montgomery Street, a Lurie-built skyscraper which is an architectural twin of 333 Michigan Boulevard, a Chicago edifice in front of which he once peddled newspapers. For years his home was a magnificently appointed floor of lavish rooms on top of Hotel Sir Francis Drake, commanding a satisfying view on all sides of Lurie-owned properties.

When the hotel eventually decided to build a cocktail lounge on that floor, Lurie looked around for another suitable aerie. Of all the possibilities he inspected, the one that most struck his fancy was a vast twelve-room, ninth-floor apartment in a handsome building at 2100 Pacific Avenue. The fact that the apartment was occupied and hence unavailable at the moment was a trifling technicality. Lurie merely purchased the whole building for $500,000.

One of his present tenants, incidentally, is San Francisco's Mayor Elmer E. Robinson, who had some difficulty getting in. "I don't know whether I want politicians in the house," the ex-newsboy grumbled after Elmer had applied for space. "They always smell up the elevators with cigar smoke."

Louis feels very strongly about elevators. He always insists on riding alone, or with friends only, to the top of his office building. Any strangers who happen to be standing in the elevator as he enters it are requested to step out and wait for another car, a suggestion that is not always met with a gracious response. "I suppose you *own* this building," is the usual reaction, to which Lurie merely nods grimly, taking a firmer bite on his especially denicotinized cigars, which are packed in Havana in boxes imprinted with his own name.

The extent of Lurie's wealth is, of course, a secret between himself, his auditors, and the income-tax department, but I imagine that Bob Hope's gag about Bing Crosby is applicable ("He doesn't pay a tax. He just calls up the Treasury and asks 'em how much they need"). One day, however, I had the eerie pleasure of watching him write out a check for exactly $1,-875,000, which, I felt reasonably certain, would immediately bounce to the height of his office windows. No such thing. Its canceled face now reposes in a glass frame in his inner sanctum, after having purchased for him a corner of Fifth and Market streets.

Only once have I seen the tycoon in financial difficulties. That came on the day he rewarded his young son Bobby with a $10 check for good behavior. Little Robert happily endorsed it and marched from store to store in the Polk Street district, trying to get the voucher cashed. He couldn't find a merchant willing to pay off to such a very little fellow carrying such a very big check.

After this day of frustration Bobby took his father on his knee that night and said softly: "Dad, I hate to tell you this —but your credit's no good!"

I'm not sure that William Saroyan, author, playwright, and genius, can be legitimately described as a San Franciscan, but we like to claim him, although he was born in Fresno and now spends most of his time in New York.

It was as a young San Franciscan, living in a room on Carl Street in the depression-racked Thirties, that Saroyan first pushed himself into the public's eye, and even, at times, its hair. This was the flamboyant, almost exhibitionistic Saroyan, who spoke and wrote so feelingly of his Armenian heritage that a wit once cracked that he suffered from "pernicious Armenia." This was the Saroyan of the thick black hair, the burning eyes, and exaggerated interest in everything and everybody, from prostitutes, in whose waiting rooms he would sit on rainy days, to Proust, whose works he used to read in the Public Library while waiting to starve to death. This was the Saroyan who used to clump around town in the only pair of shoes he owned—ski boots, because he admired their shape—and who would abruptly end a game of tennis, his favorite sport, by hitting the ball with all his might and watching it sail away over the fence, all the while laughing exultantly.

This was the Saroyan who could dash off a short story in

sixty minutes and a full-length play in six days. He lived on cigarettes and black coffee and a firm belief in himself as a writer. When his first book was rejected, he—in his own words—"rejected the rejection slip." When the editor of *Story* magazine sent him a telegram apologizing for a delay in paying him for one of his early short stories, he wired right back, in all truth: "You are not supposed to send me telegrams. I am paid to deliver them. William Saroyan."

His colossal self-esteem, as well as his undoubted flair for writing, helped him win nationwide prominence. One of the most widely circulated Saroyan tales goes back to about 1934, on a day when Bennett Cerf, the book publisher, checked into the Palace Hotel. A few minutes later the phone rang in his room, and the operator announced doubtfully: "A young man who says he's the world's greatest author is in the lobby." Answered Cerf, without hesitation: "Tell Mr. Saroyan to come right up."

Incidentally, it might come as something of a shock to John Francis Neylan, the eminent old San Francisco barrister, to know that Saroyan once included his name in a list of great contemporary writers. When somebody wondered what Bill knew about Neylan's writing, he confessed: "Well, when I worked for Postal Telegraph, I used to read the long, confidential wires he'd send to William Randolph Hearst—and I tell you they were very well written!"

Naturally Saroyan's opinion of himself is not always universally shared. In a bookstore one day I picked a copy of his *The Trouble with Tigers* off a shelf, handed it to the clerk, and asked: "How much?" Riffling through the pages, he said, "$2.50, please," but suddenly he stopped, stared at the inside cover, and hastily amended: "Oh, I'm sorry. This book is damaged. It'll be only $2.00."

The "damage," I discovered, was William Saroyan's autograph.

Another story in which Saroyan does not make the wisecrack happened on a day when he walked into a downtown barbershop and fell under the shears of a glowering barber who had nothing to say. Finally Bill, who abhors a silence as Nature abhors a vacuum, piped up brightly: "Well, guess you meet a lot of interesting characters here, hm?" "Yeah," answered the barber darkly. "You, for instance."

It was at a recital given by a gifted San Francisco pianist named Estelle Weymouth that Saroyan also failed to get in the last word. After she'd finished playing a Bach Chorale to loud applause, William arose with a grandiloquent pronouncement. "That was meaningless," he said. "Nothing but escape, pure escape. Not a note of reality in the whole piece." Another author, Haakon Chevalier, plucked at his coattails and interrupted mildly: "But don't forget, Bill, that escape is part of the reality of today."

Along with being an amateur starving Armenian, music critic, and telegraph messenger, Saroyan once worked briefly as a clerk in the grocery store of Al Conragen at Grove and Divisadero. One day, after he had achieved some recognition, he visited the store to say hello to his former employer. The news soon flashed around the neighborhood, and when Saroyan left, excited neighbors rushed into the store to ask Conragen what they had talked about.

Still singularly unimpressed by the sudden prominence of his ex-clerk, Conragen shrugged. "I was too busy to talk to him." Then he added, in a sudden burst of temper, "That Saroyan—all he does is eat up the fruit!"

Saroyan has a great gift for the quotable quote and the reportable action (columnists will always love him, no matter what the literary critics think). On a visit to his native Fresno he stopped at the street corner where he once sold newspapers in a brief moment of unoriginality. There was nobody in sight—no newsboy, no papers, no customers, nobody. As he turned to go, Saroyan sighed philosophically: "Well, that's what happens when you let somebody else run your business!"

One of Saroyan's earliest admirers was a fledgling writer named Barnaby Conrad, Jr., whose wealthy parents lived on a lush Peninsula estate, complete with swimming pool. When Bill agreed to pay him a visit there one Sunday, young Barnaby's exultation got fearfully out of hand. The longer Saroyan relaxed by the swimming pool, talking of many things, the more excited Barnaby grew—until at last he simply threw himself into the swimming pool, clothes, complexes, and all.

"What a ridiculous thing to do," growled the Senior Conrad as his sopping son splashed happily in the water. "What will Mr. Saroyan think?"

"Mr. Saroyan thinks people should do exactly what they

feel like doing," announced Mr. Saroyan, arising and jumping into the pool.

I was driving through Berkeley one day with Bill when a young man, obviously lost in thought, walked in front of my car. As he shuffled on, head down, hands in pockets, looking neither to the right nor left, Saroyan leaned out of the car and shouted: "Hello—hello there! How've you been?"

The dreamy young man didn't bother to look up. Still in his trance, he continued on his way, unaware of his near-brush with my bumpers.

"You know that guy?" I asked Saroyan.

"Thought I did," said Bill, settling back, "but now I know what it was. He reminds me of me!"

In Paris during the war I had the not inconsiderable distinction of introducing Saroyan to Ernest Hemingway at the bar of the Scribe Hotel. After they'd chatted brightly for a few minutes and Hemingway had left, I asked Bill: "You mean to say that you two had never met before?"

"We did meet once before, at a party in New York," Bill confessed, "but I don't blame him for not remembering me. After all—he was wearing a beard at the time."

Saroyan's first experience with Hollywood, long before *The Human Comedy* and *The Time of Your Life*, was short but relatively unpleasant. He was hired by a misguided major studio, where he sat around for weeks doing absolutely no writing except on the backs of weekly pay checks. But eventually somebody remembered that there was a Saroyan in the house (Hollywood joke of that era: "What is a Saroyan—

32

something that Dorothy Lamour wears?") and he was summoned by a producer.

"Well, Mr. Saroyan," said the producer briskly, "we've got a job for you. A situation that means a lot in a picture, only we can't quite capture it. It's like this. A housewife offers a starving bum a piece of apple pie. You can see he wants it, but he shakes his head and answers 'No.' Now what would you do with a situation like that?"

"I'd have the bum say 'Yes,'" snapped Saroyan, with which he walked out of the studio and returned to San Francisco.

In his earliest, brightest years as a writer Saroyan contented himself with short stories—brilliant, strange, uniquely his. Then one night Bennett Cerf took him to see his first play, a passing fancy called, as Cerf remembers it, *Ceiling Zero*. As they walked out, Saroyan spat disgustedly. "I could write a better play than that in sixty minutes." He almost succeeded in meeting that deadline. Working six days and nights (on the seventh he rested), he produced *The Time of Your Life*, which won a Pulitzer prize and the New York Critics Circle award and was eventually immortalized in celluloid.

The San Francisco *première* of the play was a sensation. Out of the tremendous ovation that followed the final curtain rose the legendary loud cries of "Author! Author!" so Star Eddie Dowling ordered the house lights up and called for Saroyan to take the stage. Long seconds passed, necks craned, but no Saroyan appeared. At last, breaking the painful silence, Dowling stepped across the footlights and blurted ex-

33

asperatedly: "Now surely he can't be out picking grapes at *this* hour!"

He wasn't. But he had gone home long before, explaining briefly to a surprised usher: "It's all right. I know how it ends."

I hope I haven't made Saroyan sound like a wisecracking, cocky smart aleck, because underneath his bravado (his volume is considerably less these days) he is warm and friendly, sincerely interested in people and what they do, and almost completely unfascinated by sham, glitter, and money.

For example, when the success of *The Time of Your Life* made him eligible for social lionization, he was invited to be guest of honor at a Nob Hill cocktail party given by Anita Howard Vanderbilt, who is intimately associated with two great fortunes. She invited a slew of her fanciest friends to meet the playwright, and everybody arrived on time except the cowardly lion.

Just as Anita was ready to give him up for lost, he shambled into her magnificent apartment, more than an hour late. "Sorry if I kept you waiting," apologized American drama's man of the year, "but honest, I thought that streetcar would *never* get here!"

As a manner of showing his disregard for money, I suppose, Bill occasionally gambles for high stakes, betting wildly, showing his cards to his opponents, and eventually losing a satisfyingly huge amount. I remember one night, though, when his own "I-don't-care" system won him a pile of cash.

He was playing stud poker with a Greek gambler in North

Beach, and after the last card was dealt, the Greek, who had a king showing, made a big bet. Saroyan, who had an ace showing, shook his head. "No use betting like that," he advised. "You can't win. I've got an ace in the hole."

The Greek, an old hand with the pasteboards, refused to be taken in by such an obvious gambit. The betting got higher and hotter, until the Greek called—whereupon Saroyan, with a shrug, turned up his second ace.

The gambler blew his top. "You lie, you lie!" he screamed. "You say you got aces back to back, and you got 'em!"

It was precisely this attitude toward money that forced Saroyan into an army uniform in World War II. When selective service began, he was exempt because he was the sole support of six relatives. Then he sold *The Human Comedy* to Metro-Goldwyn-Mayer for $60,000, and gave $10,000 to each of the six. This, of course, made the relatives self-supporting as far as the Army was concerned, and William was promptly drafted.

Out of the war emerged a new Saroyan—much older, seemingly less happy, no longer quite so sure that the world is full of beautiful people with light coming out of them. But he is still capable of the bon mot. One recent afternoon, in the Mark Hopkins lounge, he announced that he was planning to sell his Sunset District home and return to New York for good.

"What's the matter, Bill?" I asked him. "Don't you like San Francisco any more?"

"Certainly," he answered. "But tell me—do you really think it's worth a full column every day?"

I wish he hadn't said that. It's hard enough to write a daily column without that dark, Saroyan-planted thought burning in my mind.

For more than fifty years Montgomery Street has been the financial, and, in many obviously associated ways, the political hub of San Francisco.

Along this narrow, skyscraper-lined canyon, on any business day, you are almost sure to see the aforementioned Louis Lurie strolling to lunch; James Martin MacInnis, the dashing young criminal lawyer, attracting attention in his impeccable courtroom attire of black jacket, striped pants, and black homburg; Artie Samish, the lobbyist whose network of political pressure stretches across the country, looking out of a window of the Kohl Building, where he occupies two floors of offices; and Robert W. Kenny, the ex-attorney general and one-time leader of California Democrats, walking into a pub with Attorney Herbert Resner, who does well enough at the job of representing labor unions to live like a capitalist.

Kenny, who can afford to be an extreme liberal (he has a comfortable private income as well as a large law practice), makes his home in Los Angeles, but spends enough time in San Francisco to be considered One Of Us. He is a nervous, smallish man who gobbles benzedrine the way you nibble at peanuts, who likes to sit and tell jokes over dry martinis, and who might have become governor of California except for a variety of immovable objects—the largest being an incumbent named Earl Warren.

THE BIG NAMES

Although he takes politics seriously, Kenny usually gives the impression that he finds the whole business rather amusing, an attitude that might have hurt his campaign for governor. Nevertheless, he was an excellent attorney general, state senator, and judge, and is still the unofficial statewide leader of the left-wing Democrats.

It was while he was about to campaign for governor that he stood one night at the pinball machine in Shanty Malone's saloon on Sansome Street. After he had lost his tenth nickel without getting a winner, Kenny was asked by Malone: "Say, Bob, when you run for governor, what's your slogan gonna be?"

"Well," drawled Kenny, "I think it'll be—Six Balls in Every Pinball Machine."

During his term as state senator he toured California as the head of a committee appointed to help the so-called small businessman. During a hearing a stranger poked his head into the room and asked: "Say, is this the Tenney Committee?"

"No," returned Bob carefully. "Senator Jack Tenney's Committee is investigating subversive activities—and is called the 'Little Dies Committee.' This is the Kenny Committee— the 'Little Guys Committee.' "

Kenny's political demise was swift, sudden, and sure. As predicted by himself, he lost in a landslide to Governor Warren, admitting privately that some harm may have been done to his cause by what he coyly termed "the manic-progressives." He began his last speech as California's attorney gen-

37

eral at a convention of district attorneys on Catalina Island, by smiling: "Gentlemen, you are about to hear the swan song of a lame duck." And in the last national election he slammed the door on his own doghouse by supporting Henry Wallace in preference to Harry Truman.

However, seasoned California political observers never count Robert W. Kenny out of the picture no matter how unpredictable his actions. A man who can make a crowd roar with laughter has his advantages.

It seems peculiarly typical of San Francisco that the head-quarters of both Big Business and its pet hate should have been located within a few blocks of each other on the same street—Montgomery. For here, in drab contrast to the marble-halled splendor of the nearby Bank of America, was the office of Harry Bridges, president of the International Longshoremen's and Warehousemen's Union of the CIO, and for fifteen years San Francisco's most controversial figure.

To his supporters, hard-boiled, Australian-born Harry Bridges is the most slashing and forthright leader West coast labor has ever known. To those who fear his power and sus-pect his political motives, Bridges is nothing more than a long-standing threat to what they like to call "The American Way of Life" (no further explanation needed). Somewhere in between lie the obvious truths. He is an able unionist who has improved the lot of the water-front worker one hundred-fold. He is so personally honest that scores of investigators have been unable to pin a shady maneuver on him. And he is an extreme left-winger whose politics and policies usually run parallel to "the Party line."

Considered merely as one of the dominant figures in present-day San Francisco, Harry Bridges is a strong, colorful, and at times sharply amusing character. For instance, when he refused to sign a non-Communist affidavit under the Taft-Hartley Act a friend asked him whether this refusal might not indicate to the public that he is, actually, a Communist.

"How can it?" snapped Bridges. "The Supreme Court of the United States has already decided *twice* that I'm not"—which it did in voiding two strenuous attempts to deport him back to Australia as a man plotting the overthrow of the Government.

It was during the first of these deportation hearings that Estolv Ward, chief of the Bridges Defense Committee, ran across one of the best of the Bridges' legends. The story went that at one point early in his career he was shipwrecked in the Pacific and managed to struggle to safety by hanging onto a mandolin that happened to float by from the wreckage.

Ward told Bridges that he'd like to release that story in a short, "human-interest" biography of the water-front leader —a suggestion that brought a prompt and loud groan of disapproval.

"Listen, Estolv," said Bridges, "if you use that silly story they won't have to hold any deportation hearing for me. I'll just leave town by myself!"

Even those who have a multitude of reasons for opposing Bridges concede that he is an able man. During lunch one day at Jack's, Louis Lurie needled George Killion, president of the American President Lines: "George, if you were as smart as Bridges, you'd have him working for APL," to which Killion merely nodded solemnly.

At the height of a water-front strike, with the Bay virtually empty of shipping, Paul C. Smith, editor of the San Francisco *Chronicle*, invited Bridges up to his Telegraph Hill apartment, which commands a sweeping view of the harbor.

"Something has to be done about this, Harry," said Smith kiddingly, leading Bridges onto a balcony. "I used to be able to bring my guests out here during a party and show them the lights of a hundred ships at anchor. Now, as you see, there's nothing—nothing but blackness. You're ruining my view."

"Tell you what, Paul," returned Bridges. "Let me know sometime when you're having a really *big* party, and I'll tie up every ship on the Pacific coast right here in your front yard!"

It was during a Sunday brunch at Paul Smith's that Bridges first met the famed wit, Dorothy Parker. Miss Parker, it seems, had newly discovered her own social consciousness and was eager to lend a helping hand to the then still-faltering cause of labor.

"I'm going from here to Hollywood," she told Bridges in all sincerity, "and if there's anything I can do for you down there—*anything*—just let me know." Bridges shook his head and thanked her, but throughout the meal she kept asking for some slight mission to perform for him in Hollywood.

At last, as he was leaving, Bridges had an idea. He paused

at the door, turned to Miss Parker, and said: "Come to think of it, there *is* something you can do for me in Hollywood."

"Anything," repeated Miss Parker, eyes ashine. "Anything."

"Okay, get me an autographed picture of Shirley Temple," said Bridges, and out he went.

Curiously enough, it was an autographed picture sent by Shirley Temple to Bridges' daughter Betty that helped put the screen star under momentary, if ridiculous, scrutiny by the Martin Dies Committee investigating subversive activities.

Betty Bridges, by the way, often found opportunity to use her father's "bad" name to good advantage. One day, I remember, a couple of tough little kids in her neighborhood tried to steal her pet dog, Flashlight Battery, away from her. "Y'better let go," warned Betty, tugging manfully at the dog; "my father's Harry Bridges!" The kids immediately dropped their half of the pup and fled.

Bridges himself is not unaware of his own unpopularity in certain circles. At the Bal Tabarin night club I introduced him to Russell L. Wolden, the young assessor of the City and County of San Francisco, whereupon Bridges began pumping Wolden's hand heartily and beaming. "I'm certainly glad to know you. You have no idea what a great pleasure this is."

Somewhat taken back and yet slightly flattered, Assessor Wolden wondered: "Yeah? Why?"

"Because," returned Bridges happily, "a lot of people hate you too."

Today, in his mid-forties, Harry Bridges is a sallow-faced

balding man who is plagued by ulcers, recurrent revolts in his own unions, and apparently untiring efforts on the part of his enemies to label him a "Communist." Of the three, his ulcers have pained him the most, keeping him out of night clubs where he once diligently pursued his favorite indoor sport of the rumba. He now sits at home with his second wife, an ex-professional dancer, and plays chess and drinks enough milk to inspire Mrs. Bridges to join any and all organizations dedicated to the cause of lower milk prices.

In Philadelphia, during the Henry Wallace nominating convention, he was walking along a downtown street when suddenly a policeman began following him, as is not unusual with cops and Bridges.

"Hey, waitaminute, are you Harry Bridges?" shouted the officer. Bridges nodded. "Well, slow down," said the copper, "I wanna talk to you."

"Yeah? What about?" asked Bridges suspiciously.

"Ulcers," said the cop. "I got 'em too."

Thus has nationwide fame come at last to Harry Bridges.

These, then, are some of the big names in the present-day San Francisco scene—names that have come along through the recent eras of great change to blot out the Crockers and the Floods and the Sharons in the minds of a public that is fast forgetting the Bonanza headliners.

The San Franciscan of today is more interested, for instance, in the exploits of a Pierre Monteux than in the socialite descendants of the florid, hard-hitting millionaires who left their stamp on the city in the form of gingerbread mansions and ever-fading legends.

At seventy-three, the bouncy, bubbly little maestro of the San Francisco Symphony is richly enjoyed by thousands who never attend a concert. With his thick mane of black hair and his white Santa Claus mustache, he is a daily sight to see as he walks his French poodle, Fifi, around the Fairmont Hotel. Delighted passersby on the California cable car are likely to lean out from their perches and shout "Hiya, maestro!" or even, if they're among the *cognoscenti,* "Yoo-hoo, Chummy" —that, for reasons unknown to the management, being his nickname. Chummy obligingly answers any and all public greetings with a Gallic wave of his arm, a bow of his leonine head, and *voilà!* more admiring non-attenders for the San Francisco Symphony.

In 1948 the amazingly vital M. Monteux conducted one hundred and fifty-three concerts—more than any other major conductor in the country. His Symphony records sold so widely and steadily that his annual royalties from them alone totaled $40,000. He scampers out onto the stage of the Opera House at such a furious rate that there has been some talk among Symphony directors of banking the sharp turn from the rear of the stage to his podium.

In fact, I've been able to detect only two small signs of approaching age in the redoubtable maestro. A small step has been affixed to the podium to allow him to mount it more easily. And now, when he conducts from a score, which is seldom, he wears glasses.

Even his wife, Doris, an equally energetic person, is unable to explain this perpetual youth. "Maybe," she ventures, "it's because he eats a plateful of oysters, washed down with champagne, after each concert." With more than one hundred and fifty concerts on the agenda each year, you can see that M. Monteux makes deeper inroads into the oyster world than even the pearl industry.

Incidentally, Mme. Monteux is a woman of almost limitless capabilities. Along with acting as her husband's manager, press agent, and one-woman claque, she is an indefatigable speechmaker on any subject you'd care to mention. One day in 1946 I followed her with awe and admiration as she spoke on "Medicine in Russia" at the San Francisco Breakfast Club; "Commercial Aspects of Music" at Mills College; and "Football and Football Coaches" at St. Ignatius High School.

Mme. Monteux is also a patron of the arts, to the point where the Monteux apartment in the Fairmont is crammed with paintings by young San Francisco artists struggling to get ahead. Her special pet was the now successful Tom Lewis, who was "discovered" by Mme. Monteux working away in a tiny Montgomery Street garret.

After she had already bought a stack of Lewis's paintings, Mme. Monteux insisted on taking her husband up to Lewis's studio. There, she made the young painter display one after another of his works, and each time she would turn to the maestro and murmur: "Isn't that wonderful?" And each time Monteux would nod: "Yes, it's beautiful, but——"

At last his wife demanded: "Chummy, why do you always say 'It's beautiful, but'?"

"Because," twinkled Monteux, "if I don't say 'but' you'll want to buy it!"

What very few San Franciscans know is that Monteux is a man with a permanent black eye. Apparently fearing an investigation by the Un-American Activities Committee if he neglected this phase of his citizenship much longer, Monteux in the summer of 1947 decided to see his first baseball game. Accompanied by his brother-in-law, Orchestra Leader Meyer Davis, he climbed into the stands and suffered through a few innings, trying vainly to figure out the intricacies of the game.

In the fifth inning he turned to Davis and groaned: "Let's go. I'm bored."

At that point a screaming foul ball hit him just below the left eye, severely bruising his cheekbone. And now, whenever he gets overtired or rundown, his left eye turns black.

Two others whose names are solidly imprinted in the San Francisco mind are mild, quiet men intimately associated with life in prison—Warren K. Billings and Clinton Truman Duffy.

Labor and liberal forces declared a holiday of feasting and joy in 1939 when then Governor Culbert L. Olsen at last pardoned Billings and Tom Mooney, who had served twenty-three years in California prisons for the 1916 Preparedness Day bombing at Market and Steuart streets in San Francisco.

Legal observers had long cast doubt on the guilt of Mooney and Billings, and the left-wing, maintaining that the pair had simply been "crucified" as militant labor unionists, had elevated them to the emotional level previously occupied exclusively by Sacco and Vanzetti.

The pardoning ceremonies at the state capitol in Sacramento attracted caravans of unionists from San Francisco and even a smattering of movie stars, including Melvyn Douglas and Helen Gahagan, from Hollywood. Before presenting the pardon to Mooney, Governor Olsen adjusted his spectacles, carefully looked over the document, found what he was hunting for, and smiled to George T. Davis, the Mooney-Billings lawyer:

"Just wanted to make sure this pardon carries the union label. If it hadn't, I know Tom wouldn't have accepted it."

After Mooney and Billings were freed, their paths separated sharply. Mooney rather tragically seized upon the role of "labor martyr" and "Messiah," only to find, to his heartbreak, that he no longer commanded a following after he had stepped from behind bars. His actions were full of little flourishes, such as signing his old prison number instead of his name to hotel registers, and noisily canceling a gift subscription to *Life* magazine when he found out it was on a union "unfair" list.

His first appearance in San Francisco after his release was at a CIO-sponsored public rally in Civic Center. More than 40,000 laborites, well-wishers, and curiosity-seekers crowded around to hear him speak. But as he droned on and on through an hour or two of rambling, somewhat mystical ideas, the mob slowly faded away, until at the end he was speaking to only a handful of the faithful.

Tom Mooney died, less than three years after he got his freedom, unhappy, and, he felt, unwanted. Nevertheless, in the history of American labor his name will never be forgotten.

(Incidental side light: For years now people walking past 2023 Pacific Avenue have been entranced with the sight of a handsome police dog sitting in the front window. After a few seconds, however, they discover that the dog isn't alive. It's a life-sized painting of the late movie star, Rin-Tin-Tin, so lifelike that a lot of passersby imagine they hear him barking at them. The woman who owns that painting—she bought it twenty-odd years ago from a theater and figures it's handy for scaring off prowlers—is Rena Mooney, Tom's widow.)

Unlike Mooney, Warren K. Billings shunned the spotlight after his release. He married, opened a watch-repair shop on Market Street (he learned the trade in prison), and today attracts as little notice as possible. His face, however, will never be forgotten at Folsom Prison, where he spent so many years.

In the chapel of the prison is a mural of the "Last Supper," painted by a convict-artist who used several of his fellow convicts for models. And seated at the table, surrounded on one side by Dynamiter Jim McNamara and on the other by a long-dead felon, is, big as life, Warren K. Billings.

The warden of one of the world's largest and most overcrowded penitentiaries might reasonably be expected to be

47

a burly, hard-spoken disciplinarian, packing a gun as he shoulders his way through the prison yard and living in constant fear of an outbreak among his prisoners.

Warden Clinton T. Duffy of San Quentin fits no part of that description, however. A slight grayish man who wears glasses, he looks more like a librarian than the absolute ruler of some 5000 lawbreakers. He seldom speaks of brutality or of restrictive measures to be used against the few prisoners who get out of line. His main concern at "Q," as the prison is known among its inmates, is in rehabilitation, in ways and means of transforming prisoners into potentially useful citizens after their release.

As a result, Warden Duffy, unlike his predecessors, can walk alone, unarmed and unguarded, among hundreds of prisoners, greeting scores of them by name, discussing work and the weather with others, listening to complaints and suggestions with courtesy and attentiveness.

A typical Duffy story concerns the time, a few years ago, he was considering turning San Quentin's huge dining halls into cafeterias. When I asked him why, he explained simply: "Well, it'll give the boys a choice of food. The way it is now, they have to eat any old thing that is slapped down in front of them."

And whereas things like this don't happen at "Q" *every* day, this did happen there on a recent Christmas Eve: a Negro prisoner walked up to Duffy, suddenly produced a pair of dice, shook them expertly, and grinned: "Shoot you for five days, Warden!"

THE BIG NAMES

But perhaps the neatest capsule description of his gentleness came from an associate who told me one day: "Clint is so kind-hearted he has to surround himself with 'No' men."

This is Clinton T. Duffy, the unusual warden—justifiably a celebrity among the unusual people of Baghdad-by-the-Bay.

6.

ONE SUNDAY AFTERNOON

Mr. and Mrs. San Francisco are drawn irresistibly to the sea
on a sunny Sunday.

They drive in droves through Golden Gate Park, straining
for that first glimpse of the water. They spread out along the
Beach, they cluster in the Cliff House, they stare at Seal
Rocks with anguished eyes as though they wish they could
frolic there too. They range along the Marina and look at the
sails in Yacht Harbor and lose themselves in Mitty-like
dreams of galleons and doubloons along the Spanish Main.

For San Franciscans, all of them—the clerks, the housewives, the bookies, the bankers—are sprinkled ever so slightly
with salt spray, and on Sunday they go down to the sea in
cars to fill their lungs with the tang of their heritage.

In a way, it's the traditional Sunday in Baghdad-by-the-
Bay. The guy with the hangover gulping down a creamy New

ONE SUNDAY AFTERNOON

Orleans fizz at the Cliff House, the broker rolling up the pants legs of his Montgomery Street business suit to wade in the surf, the chorine flexing her handsome legs as she pumps a bicycle through Golden Gate Park—these characters are not necessarily of 1949. Their counterparts were doing exactly the same things in 1889.

How do I remember that? I'm a San Franciscan. I was born with memories.

But there's more to Sunday in San Francisco than the weekly traffic jam caused by people with a single thought in thousands of automobiles. And in my own perverse way I like the other side of the picture—where time stands still in the hush of a deserted street.

I enjoy the Sabbath silence of the financial district, noisy with a new dimension of unpeopled space. Along the empty sidewalks only vagrant scraps of paper scud before the wind that, on other days, toys with men's hats and women's skirts. The imposing skyscrapers suddenly look lost and childish without the people who make them tick between long week ends. What is more useless than a skyscraper on Sunday? Even the Russ Building, so domineering and dignified, broods alone, like a big plaything cast aside.

In the produce district the timeless shadows lay long over the squat old buildings, and only a cat prowls slowly between the neatly stacked boxes. On block after block of San Francisco's larder Sunday has hung its padlock. Vanished the trucks, gone the workers. Only the buildings sleep there,

51

showing their age and the cracks in their surface as the unbroken sun beats down. Suddenly it seems like a city of the dead—this city within a city that feeds the city six days a week.

Sunday is quiet and kindly on the Embarcadero. The big ships doze at the end of their lines, as though the water were tepid enough to make them sleepy. The saloons are empty and the bartenders stand outside the doors, talking to children. Only the Ferry Building seems unaware that this is the Sabbath. Every day is Sunday now, for this sad old pile of gray—dead and useless except for the clock that goes ticking on when all else is gone.

Along O'Farrell, Eddy, and Ellis the pasty-faced people who are chained to tiny apartments venture out to the sidewalks, like prisoners at the end of their short ropes. From their kitchenettes they drag little white chairs, and there they sit in the sun, close to their front doors, as though they might have to dart back into their holes at a moment's notice. The oldsters squat on the stone stairs, blinking and uncomfortable, and gaze down at the warm pavement, for deep inside they know the sun is only for the rich.

Only in Fillmore's "Little Harlem" are the sidewalks teeming with people in their Sunday best and worst, lounging, talking, standing in busy knots. A tenement is bad enough during the week, but on a sunny Sunday it is unbearable.

Sunday in the far reaches of the Mission and Visitacion Valley and Butchertown has a special flavor—not of San

Francisco, but of any small town in any era of the American story.

On street corners and between houses the kids lazily throw a baseball while little girls in pink dresses watch from their porches and follow the flight of the ball, back and forth, back and forth. In the distance you can hear the oddly nostalgic clatter of a lawn mower. Under a shade tree a man and his wife are washing their ten-year-old car until it gleams. A boy on a reluctant bike moves past in a dream. The only thing missing is the bang of a screen door, and your ears strain for it until you remember: there are few flies in San Francisco.

Here and there on the Mission hillsides you see the old houses that stand as mirrors for your memory. The shingled roofs, the plate-glass window that marks the "front" room, the wide porch where ghosts sit and rock in wicker chairs, the brick chimneys—monuments, all, in today's cemetery of white stucco cubicles.

And suddenly you remember with a strange sharpness the old, unhurried days, when these houses were fresh and new. When there were wide-open spaces for more houses you thought would never come to crowd you in. When the peace and quiet of a sunny Sunday didn't come just once or twice in a year of weeks—but seemed to hang heavy and sweet over the world every day.

7.

CHINATOWN, OUR CHINATOWN

The biggest Chinatown outside of Asia. Where 30,000 people are crowded into a few blocks, so they can attract tourists and disease. Chinatown. Beloved indulgently and condescendingly by the rest of San Francisco—as long as its inhabitants stay in their own places and make no attempt to cross the invisible boundaries into the "white" city.

Chinatown. Contributing more than its share of color and culture since the earliest days of Baghdad-by-the-Bay—and yet never represented in the City Hall, although its sizable vote (mostly Democratic) is ardently wooed by every politician. Strange little transplanted world of bald-headed women who still wear the costume of their forefathers, of "sharp" university graduates who want something better than their fathers got, of bright-eyed childen who play in the dank alleys and somehow remain charming and flowerlike.

Contrasts, confusion, conflicts. Neon and chromium fronts on buildings that reek of the ages inside. A million dollars' worth of oriental treasures in a "Family Association" meeting room, opening onto a balcony that overlooks flat rooftops covered with drying fish. Phony pagoda corners on houses, a delight to the tourist but deplored by the young Chinese architects who want to see their section modernized as long as they're restricted to it.

"Traditional" Chinatown, its ancient customs revered by all. But the opium smokers are dragged into court and the gamblers are trailed unceasingly by the cops and for years there wasn't even a pinball machine to be found because some Chinese might bet on them.

Chinatown. You return from every trip through its byways with some new scrap of information, some new acquaintance.

Albert Chow, the unofficial mayor, power in the Chinese Chamber of Commerce, a Number-1 man in the ruling clique known as the Chinese Six Companies. It was smiling Albert who took President Truman and his family into a then new Grant Avenue restaurant called Kuo Wah—whose slogan in loud letters shortly thereafter brazened: "Only Chinese Restaurant in San Francisco Visited by President Truman and His Family." Albert Chow—whose brother Jack is part owner of a rival Grant Avenue restaurant, the Jade Palace.

Chingwah Lee, the art collector, who played one of the leading roles in *The Good Earth* and is always in demand by Hollywood. Chester Gann, the "Japanese" villain in many a wartime film, now running a camera shop on Grant Avenue because the end of the war meant the end of his usefulness as a celluloid bad man. Johnny Kan, Chinatown's good-will ambassador, who has introduced hundreds of "outsiders" to the inside of his district and made them understand and sympathize with the way his people live.

Dolly Gee, for years the ever-grinning manager of Bank of America's Chinatown branch, staffed completely with Chinese. T. A. Soong, brother of China's once-powerful and still-wealthy T. V. Soong, who runs the Bank of Canton (he is chauffeured to work by a major in the Chinese Army, and when he walks into his establishment each morning the employees rise and bow gravely). Charlie Low, once a bus boy, now the wealthy polo-playing owner of a night club that made good because it was the first to feature Chinese chorines displaying bare legs—to the endless dismay of Chinatown's elders.

Chinatown. Where you instantly label yourself a "tourist" if you order chop suey, an American invention. Where the clock in the Western Union office tells you what time it is at the moment in China. Where an Italian newsboy named Chester has been peddling papers at the corner of Jackson and Grant Avenue for so many years that he can now speak Chinese—with an Italian accent. Where a spot called the Shanghai Low casts modesty and even credibility to the winds by advertising: "A Visit to Our Café Is the Equal of a Visit to China." Where Lum & Co. operate a store at 1000 Grant Avenue that is called, for absolutely no reason at all, "The Italian Grocery."

CHINATOWN, OUR CHINATOWN

Fascinating, the Chinese. They call San Francisco *"Dia Fow,"* which means "big town," and the old-timers still refer to Grant Avenue, the main street, by its original name of "Dupont Gai."

One of their favorite dishes is a sort of gruel known as "jook," as prepared by Sam Wo in a tall, narrow three-story building on a side street. Sam's jook joint does well. Every night there is the ceaseless clatter of soup bowls, the ceaseless singsong of many wagging tongues. Every night Sam Wo sells almost a thousand bowls of jook.

The names on the street signs, mellifluous, monosyllabular, sometimes amusing. The Sing Fat Co., for instance, where there is no Mr. Sing Fat (the term merely means "Expanding Prosperity"). Likewise, an undertaking parlor called "Wing Sang Co."—another way of saying "Everlasting Life." And as for the drugstore named "Chaan Ning Hong Co."—that means "Place of Abounding Longevity."

The classic Chinese laundryman—obviously ready to wash your clothes at any time, day or night, as witness the Moonlight Laundry on Bush, the Starlight Laundry, and the Sunshine Laundry. To say nothing of Wo Shing and Sum Wo.

Even the ancient "No tickee, no washee!" wheeze lives on in the minds of San Francisco's Chinese, but with delicate, sardonic improvements. For example, when the police recently announced a clamp down on Chinese lotteries, an ancient Oriental refused a customer by grinning in outrageous pidgin English: "Solly. No tickee, cop watchee!"

But perhaps the most celebrated example of the Chinese

sense of humor was this widely reprinted sign that first appeared in a laundry: "You ask credit, I no give, you get sore. You ask credit, I give, you no pay, I get sore. Better you get sore."

Chinatown has played two historic roles—one of them involuntary—in the legends of San Francisco labor. The first union label was invented to distinguish white-made cigars from the Chinese variety. And the first organized strike in San Francisco was staged by Chinese almost one hundred years ago. A crew was putting together a Montgomery Street building made of granite blocks shipped from China and marked in Chinese so they could be fitted together properly. One of the wiser coolies suddenly realized that only he and his countrymen could read the markings, so he declared a strike and won an immediate raise.

Then there is the celebrated tale of the green hats. In the 1920s Foreman & Clark, the men's clothiers, opened a branch store in Chinatown. Its manager, Gene Engle, now a successful restaurateur, one day featured a very special sale of green hats, and was appropriately amazed when the first day passed without a single transaction. He tried again the second day, with the same result. On the third day a Chinese friend tipped him off. According to ancient tradition, when a Chinese wears a green hat, it means his wife has been unfaithful.

Problems, always problems. One of the nastier ones involves two or three "white" landlords who own apartment houses on the fringe of Chinatown. But they refuse to rent to whites. They'd rather rent, at gouging figures, to well-to-do Chinese caught helplessly between overcrowded Chinatown and the restrictive covenants. One Chinese who pays a fabulous rental for a miserable apartment sighed to me one night: "Every month I perform the neat trick of holding my nose— and paying through it at the same time."

More appetizing is the story of Suey Chong, who runs a trinket shop on Grant Avenue. He could scarcely believe his goggled eyes one day when into his little store strode Mrs. Franklin D. Roosevelt. She made some purchases and paid him with a personal check, which the awe-struck Suey refused to cash. Instead, he had it framed and hung it in his shop. Months later, to Suey Chong's in Chinatown, came a letter from the White House, asking him to please cash Mrs. Roosevelt's check so she could balance her account.

Incidentally, W. F. Doon, an ex-president of the Six Companies, recently named his new son Truman Doon, and shortly after received a one-dollar bill from Washington inscribed: "To Truman Doon from Harry S. Truman." Doon immediately had the dollar insured—for $1000.

Chinatown. If it weren't for its spell and its people, these "it could only happen here" stories wouldn't happen. To explain:

On a crowded Kearny Street bus one afternoon two Chinese businessmen were talking to each other, loudly and volubly, in their native tongue. Suddenly one of them sneezed. The other hastily said *"Gesundheit!"* after which the conversation in Chinese continued.

Then, one recent Monday night Dr. Robert F. Gobar of Daly City drove into town for his regular weekly meal at his favorite Chinese restaurant. To his surprise he found the place closed, although it had never before been closed on a Monday. After he had banged on the door for a few minutes, the Chinese proprietor poked his head out and said: "Sorry, we're not open tonight." Then, as Dr. Gobar registered surprise, he added: "Yom Kippur, you know."

Yes, it's Chinatown and its people that, more than any other single factor, make San Francisco "different." The proof came to me strikingly one day recently when I walked into a Chinese grocery on Stockton Street. Inside, the Chinese clerk was in the middle of a conversation with a white man obviously from Texas.

And—this is what makes San Francisco "different"—the one who sounded like a "foreigner" was the Texan.

8.

ALL THROUGH THE NIGHT

Famed are the nights of San Francisco—famed for the stuff of which storybooks are made. It's not necessarily the night life of cabarets and pubs and dancing and drunks. It's more a feeling and a mood. Of activity that doesn't stop when the sun goes down, of a city that never quite goes to sleep, of people wandering restlessly through the shadows—drawn not by a search for the dark and prosaic pleasures of the night, but by the mystery and beauty of a city with its shades drawn over soft lights.

San Francisco, the city born with the soul of a harridan, is more herself when the street lights flick up on her hills and in her valleys. The night becomes her. Suddenly there are the implications of melodrama in the blackness of the Bay, splotched here and there by the amber reflections from the bridges. Sharply, you can hear the sighing of water among

61

the rotting timbers of the piers that bite, like a row of jagged teeth, into the harbor. The cable slots sing more loudly along the quiet streets, and the fog drifts in and out of alleys, turning them into stage sets for a play that needs no actors.

Only at night do you seem to get the old feeling—Novelist Frank Norris always felt it—that "anything can happen in San Francisco."

Early evening. Far out in the Pacific the sun has punched its time clock and called it a day, and in Baghdad-by-the-Bay the nightly game of make-believe begins. All over town the brassy neons flare up to splash their quick, cheap paint over tawdry fronts you pass unheeding during the day; with their lights glowing, the tiniest bars, the most uninspired restaurants take on a certain glamor. Traffic pours both ways through its endless locks of red and green signals—for the clerk and the salesman must get home to their tiny apartments, and those who live in the night are being drawn downtown by the invisible magnet, by the unspoken invitation, the maybe, the could be, the who knows what the night may bring?

Then comes the sanctified two-hour hush as the city settles down to feed itself.

The smell of cooking seeps up and down the halls of a thousand apartment houses that all look alike and smell alike—from Bush Street to Broadway. The restaurants fill the chill air with a greasy perfume, and, with a city-wide clatter of knives and forks, the great ritual is solemnly enacted. After which, satisfied for a while, Mr. and Mrs. San Francisco begin looking around for something to do, for the night is valuable, its few hours a precious commodity.

The pageant of the night begins with relative dignity.

The neighborhood movies fill slowly with the people from next door and around the corner, who'd be darned if they'd stand in line to see a first-run show on Market Street. The taverns out in the avenues come to life as the couples desert their cramped apartments for a drink with their neighbors, and the atmosphere is almost as clubby as that in an English pub. In Chinatown's "Fish Alley" ancient yellow-skinned men gather under cruelly bright lights in tiny shops to play mah-jongg—and in "Little Italy" the Italianos, fierce of breath and mustache, begin their nightly games of *bocce* ball.

The "flying squads" of the Police Department fan out across the city in their purposefully nondescript automobiles—out into the Mission to look for car thieves, along the streets of "Little Harlem" with its marijuana peddlers, through the dark and dusty Western Addition to watch for housebreakers.

In the tenderloin joints of Mason and Taylor and Eddy and Turk the sailors perch warily on stools, their eyes darting from ankle to ankle, and the lone girls, the "sea gulls," patrol Market Street, their eyes as sparkly as soda water.

But for some the night is as day, for work is work, no matter when you do it. Irritable in the wet fog, the traffic cops swing their arms to keep warm, and along Powell the flower vendors turn up their collars, shivering at the job of selling the products of sun and heat. To each customer who complains about his weak drink the bartender complains about his flat feet, and the waiters lug their trays between the crowded tables and wish they'd decided to be shoe salesmen, instead. And the cabdrivers look dismally through their flick-flacking windshield wipers and think about home and a warm bed and mentally curse the conventioneers who ask: "Hey, cabby, where can a guy find a gal in this town?"

On the Skid Road of Howard and Mission the beggars shuffle off as though they had someplace to go, some choice between starving or freezing. The pitch for "A dime fer a cuppacoffee" changes, by rote, to "A quarter for a place to sleep, mister?"—and how can you say no, even though you know both the dime and the quarter will go for the same thing: a slug of sherry that brings a momentary warmth at least.

Around midnight the San Francisco nocturne begins to take shape.

Now there is a semi-silence in the air, for the theaters are almost empty, the bowlers have packed their shoes away, the bridge games have broken up (along with a marriage or two), and the night is left to its rightful and wrongful heirs.

In the saloons the tempo is quickened, for only an hour or two remain to get the job done. Deserted suddenly are the streets of Chinatown, and dimly lit Waverly Place becomes the setting for a tong war in shadow play. Along the Embarcadero the great ships sleep at the end of their lines, moving ever so slightly, as in a dream.

ALL THROUGH THE NIGHT

To the counterpoint of whimpering foghorns drama flashes suddenly in the night, jutting up here and there over the city in tiny spurts that die almost as they are born. Now, in the half-world of post-midnight, you know things are going on. In an ordinary-looking house in the Richmond District—a poker game with the stakes in the thousands, played by men whose faces are in police files all over the country. In a handsome white home in the Lakeside District—an abortion. In a madame's ornate mansion on Pine Street—a state official risking his career for a couple of champagne hours. And in a hundred midtown apartment houses and hotels, where the lights flash on and off behind drawn shades at regular intervals, and the taxicabs come and go as though on a schedule.

Then the cavalcade goes into its last, long phase.

The bandleaders, the bartenders, and the girls head for the late restaurants, glad their jobs are over, but in no hurry to call it a night; their sleep begins at dawn. A lone "Owl" streetcar rattles along Market, forlorn, decrepit, and listing. The big neon signs have gone cold and dead, and there is no longer competition for the filigree tracery of the bridges, the fog-muffled beacon of Alcatraz.

The night rules with black finality over the residential districts, over Pacific Heights and St. Francis Wood, where the silence is so thick you can hear it. Soon the only lights are those high in the financial district skyscrapers, as sleepy-eyed janitresses finish their last rites in preparation for the coming day. The garbage collectors, fresh from sleep, begin hauling away yesterday's debris, singing loud Italian songs and rattling their tin cans with the assurance of those who know their jobs are secure—who would want them?

Then the first faint smudge appears in the sky behind the East Bay hills, and in the hushed unreality of a moment the magic of the night disappears in thin, cold air.

9.

MEN, WOMEN, AND JUDGES

For all its reckless past San Francisco today is a pretty law-abiding city. For one thing, there are no organized mobs of importance; the Police Department, jealously guarding its own inalienable rights and privileges, sees to that. The book-makers are hounded, with laughable intensity, by a righteous newspaper whose managing editor is an inveterate bettor. Only one madame, a wise woman who obviously knows where all the best bodies are buried, operates, more or less openly, in a crenelated mansion on a busy downtown street. It is even rather difficult, unless you're on your toes every minute, to find a place that will serve you a drink after the official 2 A.M. closing hour.

Not that San Francisco has become completely dull. There is still a high potential for wickedness, ready to flourish in a ready-made atmosphere of tolerance for those who skirt the law without injuring too many people in the delicate process. If you want to go to enough trouble, you can still bet on a horse without going to the track. "Call" girls roam the night from hotel to hotel, operating inside a network of bellboys and taxi drivers. Grocery stores act as fronts for petty bootleggers who'll see that you get that bottle of scotch at four in the morning. And your parking tag? "Give it to me, I'll fix it," is a sentence that falls easily and truthfully from the lips of hundreds who have a little "juice" and like to use it.

But as you can see, this is pretty tame stuff compared with the storied nights of the Barbary Coast and political bosses whose corruption literally crumpled a city hall and who bribed and angled so openly that the smell was even detectable in Washington. This is most certainly not the San Francisco of the "Coast" that a newspaperman described in the 1870s as "that sink of moral pollution whose reefs are strewn with human wrecks and into whose vortex is constantly drifting barks of moral life, while swiftly down the whirlpool of death go the sinking hulks of the murdered and the suicide!"

That's what the man said.

This temperate calm that has fallen uneasily over San Francisco might be because of a sudden lack of ambition and inventiveness among lawbreakers. It might also be owing to a plodding police chief who doesn't smoke or drink and goes to Mass three times a day. Or even to as upstanding a body of judges as can be found under an elective system that forces these august, supposedly impartial personages to become politicians, and therefore to make as many friends as possible in order to insure re-election every few years. Under these circumstances it is easy to understand why an occasional traffic tag is fixed and why Justice sometimes coughs discreetly and looks the other way. The American Way, I might add.

There are some real honeys among San Francisco's judges. One of the most beloved, one of the most "San Francisco" (the word is often used as an adjective) is ageless, benevolent, white-haired Matthew I. Brady—just plain "Matt" to practically everybody. Matt has been in politics since he was old enough to kiss a baby, instead of being kissed as one himself. He was a police judge and then district attorney for what seemed like centuries to everyone who tried to defeat him (twenty-four years, to be exact). And when he was finally beaten by young Edmund Gerald "Pat" Brown in 1944 he bounced right back as a municipal judge.

Matt has a commendable compassion for those less fortunate than he. For years he "kept" three gentlemen who would wait for him daily on Kearny Street, always in the same positions: one on top of a fire hydrant, the second on an ash can, and the third on the car fender. One day the judge was surprised to find only the latter two in position. "Where's the fellow who controls the hydrant?" he asked the guardian of the ash can. "He's got the flu, Judge," was the answer, "but I'll take his money to him." That was good enough for Matt. He met the usual pay roll.

I remember being in court one day when a particularly woozy-eyed Skid Rowgue appeared before him after a hard night in the drunk tank. As he swayed back and forth, emitting slight but pitiable moans, Judge Brady looked down and asked solicitously: "My good man, do you have a hangover?" The defendant shook his throbbing head. "No, Your Honor," he sighed, "me, I got a holdover." When the judge looked blank, the sufferer explained: "There is a difference, see? You wake up sober, but feeling awful—that's a hangover. You wake up feeling awful, but still drunk—that's a holdover. I got a holdover."

For thus contributing to his vocabulary Judge Brady did the right thing. "Dismissed!"

However, even Matt can be pushed too far. One morning recently a saloonkeeper he has known for years was haled into his courtroom on a charge of being inebriated to the point of intoxication. Drunk. "How come you let this happen to you, a citizen of standing in the community?" asked the judge sternly. "Well, it was like this, Matt," began the unhappy pub owner, whereupon Judge Brady snapped: "Let's get one thing straight. When I'm at your bar, you can call me Matt. When you're at *my* bar, you call me judge!"

As far as I can see, Judge Brady, who is seventy-three, will go on forever as a San Francisco institution. Nevertheless, there are certain small signs that he has lost the first flush of youth. One day he displayed some annoyance when Public Defender Gerald Kenny handed him a document to read. "Look, Jerry," he complained, "you know I can't read this small type without my glasses."

"There they are," said Kenny, pointing to the spectacles. "Right there on the desk in front of you."

"They are?" returned Matt, groping for them. "Oh. I couldn't see them without my glasses."

The "queen" of the Superior Court is Judge Theresa Meikle. Tessie, as you soon learn to call her, is a surprisingly sweet, unsophisticated woman—seemingly unhardened by years on end on the bench. Her decisions are wise, temperate, and just. In fact, the only time I recall hearing her become even slightly rattled was the day she wound up her remarks to a new jury by declaring solemnly: "And here I sit like the Statue of Liberty, with my eyes blindfolded, holding the scales of Justice!"

The attractive (but unmarried) Tessie has a disregard for established courtroom procedure too. Old bailiffs and seasoned court attachés could hardly believe their eyes or ears one afternoon when Judge Meikle, learning that it was Attorney Joseph Haughey's birthday, turned brightly to the jury and instructed: "Ladies and gentlemen of the jury, you will please arise and sing 'Happy Birthday' to Mr. Haughey." Musical history was thereupon made.

But my favorite Tessie Meikle story concerns the time she confided to her Cathedral Apartment neighbor, Mrs. Zach Coblentz: "You know, your husband snores so loudly I can hear him right through the wall." Mrs. Coblentz started to murmur apologies, but Judge Meikle gushed right on: "It's wonderful. It's so reassuring to know there's a man in the house!"

Then we have the mighty mite of the San Francisco judi-

71

ciary, Judge Twain Michelsen, a small, precise, and somewhat delicate man who doesn't smoke, doesn't drink, grows flowers on his Pacific Avenue rooftop as a hobby, and is a strict vegetarian ("Never the Twain shall meat" is a deathly phrase someone coined about him).

For years Judge Michelsen was chiefly known around town as the man who would deliver a long, ringing speech on the evils of narcotics at the drop of a toastmaster's gavel. Not, originally, that the young Twain was any more concerned about dope than a half-dozen other vices. It was simply that, having decided on a political career, he called upon the late great manipulator of political machinery, Tom Finn, and asked him for a safe, over-all subject for public speechmaking.

"Talk against the dope habit, son," grunted Tom. "I ain't never yet found anybody who's on record in favor of it."

Twain Michelsen then and there went on record as the implacable foe of narcotics in all its forms.

But it was as a municipal judge, meting out justice to the drinking habitués of Skid Road, that Michelsen came to everyone's attention as a more than ordinarily noteworthy bench warmer.

There was the day he delivered a heart-to-heart talk to three Skid Rowgues who'd become regular customers of his court.

"What you men need," advised the goodhearted judge, "is a change of atmosphere. Get away from Third and Howard once in a while. Forget the muscatel for a day. Go out to

Golden Gate Park, for instance, and breathe the clean, pure air and look at the beautiful flowers. It'll do worlds of good for you."

Two of the Three Muscatels agreed that that wasn't such a bad idea and hitched a ride out to the Park—where the vigilant coppers promptly arrested them as vagrants and ran them back to the jailhouse.

Next day they appeared again before Judge Michelsen, to whom one Skidkid looks pretty much like the next. He listened to the charges, then waggled a finger at the defendants and tsk-tsked: "Arrested in Golden Gate Park, eh? How many times must I tell you men not to hang around places frequented by women and children? Next time this happens, I'm going to have to give you jail sentences!"

The two Skid Rowgues, sighing deeply at life's perversities, shuffled out. At the courtroom door one of them paused long enough to crack sarcastically to his buddy: "See? I *toldja* we shoulda changed to our sport clothes!"

On another unforgettable occasion Judge Michelsen's sensitive nostrils were offended more than somewhat by the fragrance emanating from his charges. Not wishing to insult the bleary, dreary prisoners, for he is, after all, a kindly man, he merely commented sharply from the bench: "This courtroom smells something *fierce!* Don't the janitors ever clean up around here?"

That night the Hall of Justice cleanup crew, wishing to forestall possible complaints, really went to work, mopping, scrubbing, and sterilizing for hours.

Next morning at ten the judge mounted the bench, sniffed the air for long, silent minutes, glared at the Skid Roaders arrayed before him, and then shouted: "For Heaven's sake, somebody open the windows—quickly! What have you men been drinking *this* time—*Clorox?*"

Some time later, in an effort to neutralize the various offending perfumes, the judge installed a chemical deodorizer on the side of his bench. But even that failed to clear the air perceptibly one morning when five members of Howard Street sherry society stood before him. Wrinkling his nose delicately, Judge Michelsen asked, purely rhetorically: "Which one of these men smells so horribly?"

There was a short lull—whereupon the meekest member of the quintet, after furtively glancing around, raised his hand and piped: "Me, Judge."

Somewhat taken aback by such self-condemnation, the judge rallied sufficiently to say: "Well, just for your frankness I'm dismissing you. But leave the courtroom hurriedly."

The Skid Rowgue scuttled happily out the door. A few seconds later the judge, leaning a little closer toward his deodorizer, was heard to remark pensively to no one in particular: "Hm. I wonder if that man could have been deceiving me?"

For all these quirks, which are, after all, human and likable, Judge Michelsen is a fearless, courageous public servant who sticks firmly, even stubbornly to his principles. Once he had a long and heated row with Deputy Police Chief Michael J. Riordan over the police methods of solving the downtown traffic riddle—no part of which the judge could bring himself to condone. After days of futile argument Chief Riordan at last confessed in defeat: "I'm Irish and a drinking man. Judge Michelsen is Scandinavian and he doesn't drink. If I could only get him over to a bar, we could settle the whole traffic situation in no time!"

Judges sometimes have their troubles with the lawyers who disport in their courtrooms.

The erratically brilliant William Herron, finally disbarred a few years ago, made a historic appearance before Superior Judge Sylvain Lazarus one day—creating an incident that is still chewed over with relish whenever judges and barristers get together. In the midst of arguing a case before Lazarus, Herron suddenly began showering compliments on the judge, to his obvious embarrassment.

"Your Honor," he intoned, "no judge on the bench today has your intelligence, your breadth of judgment, your high moral principles." Brushing past the judge's mumbled "Oh, come now," Herron insisted: "You are a man among men, sir, a gentleman of culture and refinement, without a doubt——" Demanded Lazarus: "Mr. Herron, I must ask you to get on with the case." Herron bowed suavely. "Let me finish, Your Honor. In short, as Sir Francis Bacon said to Lord Ellenborough"—here Herron raised his index finger for dramatic emphasis—"*if* you knew a little law, you'd be a great judge!"

Which reminds me of the case of the equally brilliant but even more erratic San Francisco lawyer who today is also disbarred. He scored his most famous court victory defending a man against a charge of criminal assault. While the prosecution was ranting at the jury of six men and six women he sat in his chair and drowsed. Then it was his turn. He shuffled to the jury box with a suspicious, weaving motion, and draped himself over the rail and mumbled: "Us ———— men gotta stick together!" Then he ambled back to his chair and passed out again. The jury of six men and six women failed to reach a verdict. They were split—six to six.

And perhaps this would be as good a place as any to mention Superior Judge Preston Devine, who, along with being a jurist of high repute, has contributed his bit to the deathless lore of San Francisco. In the middle of a fish dinner one day he was suddenly seized with inspiration. Grabbing a menu, he scribbled on its back an "Ode to Fisherman's Wharf," which has already taken its place alongside Wallace Irwin's "Tellygraft Hill" and Gelett Burgess's "Ballad of the Hyde Street Grip" in the hearts of those who love Baghdad-by-the-Bay. It goes:

> Best of all I love to grab
> A double-header glass of crab,
> Tomato sauce and squeeze a bit
> Of lemon over me and it!

10.

THAT, TOO, WAS THE WAR

World War II hit Baghdad-by-the-Bay like a ton of block busters.

Overnight the self-contained, self-satisfied city whose population had stood absolutely still for a decade was transformed into a major Port of Embarkation, a vital war industries center, a possible primary target for enemy action.

The town that, traditionally, welcomed tourists, but was suspicious of strangers who hung around, found itself swamped under hordes of war workers and thousands of servicemen. In the twinkling of a raised eyebrow there was a housing shortage within the city's inflexible boundaries. Prices whistled into the stratosphere like a new, secret weapon. Every night in the hectic weeks following December 7 was crazy with rumors of Japanese planes overhead, Japanese submarines off the Golden Gate.

But, as usual, San Franciscans soon found something to laugh and joke about. The first "black-out" exercises. Fortunately, the enemy was in no position to take advantage of the brilliant display of exterior lighting that followed the first signal to black out. While Civilian Defense chiefs blew their tops with loud, popping sounds, San Franciscans responded to the call as though they were celebrating the centennial of Thomas Alva Edison.

It was at this time that then Mayor Angelo J. Rossi achieved fleeting immortality. Hounded by reporters to explain why his city staged a festival of light when it should have been black, Angelo shrugged and smiled:

"Well—no bombs fell, did they?"

But the black-out incident that sticks most closely in my mind happened a couple of "exercises" later. With the city pretty snugly under a blanket of darkness, sudden mysterious flashes of light were seen gleaming from a window high in a hilltop apartment house. They looked like a code message. Swiftly the guardians of security surrounded the place, and a squad broke into the guilty apartment.

They found that a large group of people had been having a party there when the black-out siren sounded. They obediently turned out the lights and sat in the pitch blackness for long, boring minutes. Then one after another tiptoed into the kitchen to get a bottle of beer from the refrigerator. Those mysterious "code" flashes were merely the light in the icebox—as the door was sporadically opened and closed.

THAT, TOO, WAS THE WAR

In retrospect it is painfully easy to see that the bombs that fell on Pearl Harbor destroyed a good part of San Francisco too. Not just in overcrowding and inflation; those twin evils were hardly peculiar to a single city. What was swept away in the debris, to return slowly, was a certain expansiveness of spirit, a long-established understanding of other races and people, a quality that was reflected most obviously in good food, good drinks, and good living.

During the short (in the scheme of things) war years certain saloonkeepers boastfully became millionaires at the expense of servicemen; the black market swallowed up once-useful citizens; some restaurants sacrificed years of reputation on the altar of the quick buck. In short, a whole tradition went down the drain, and a city's name was tarnished. Not a pretty sight to see in a world-famed metropolis noted for a "special" something.

And it was "too bad, but inevitable," they said, that the loyal Japanese-Americans should have to suffer along with the guilty. The twisted ships had hardly settled on the bottom at Pearl Harbor when San Francisco's large Nisei colony began to feel the blow. Crowds of sailors on Grant Avenue hurled rocks through the windows of Japanese curio stores, especially those which immediately displayed placards reading "I Am Proud to Be an American." In the confusion, Chinese were beaten up and eventually took to wearing lapel buttons that insisted: "I Am Chinese" in big black letters. The telephone in my office rang night and day with canards about trusted Japanese gardeners who suddenly turned out to be admirals, and houseboys who were hauled away to internment camps, hissing at their quaking employers: "Someday I come back—and when I come back, I kill you!"

One of the less vicious fables concerned an air-raid drill in a Peninsula elementary school. At a signal from the teacher the children were supposed to duck under their desks. So the teacher gave the sign, watched as the children disappeared, and then bent down to slide under her own desk. But already there, according to the tale, was a grinning Japanese child.

Slightly more amusing, perhaps, was the story that allegedly happened December 8, 1941, in a nearby rural school district where the children are picked up in a bus on the way to school. After several white children had boarded, the teacher decided it was time for a little lecture. "At the next stop," she said, "we're picking up Yoshio. Now, I know we're all excited about what happened yesterday, but remember, he's an American, just like the rest of us. So be sure you treat him like one of us."

At the next stop there was an uncomfortable silence as little Yoshio climbed aboard. For a few minutes not a word was spoken in the bus. Then Yoshio piped up. "Well," he said cheerily, "guess we sure beat the heck out of *you* guys yesterday!"

An incident that still rankles in the heart of all good Stanford men occurred several years before Pearl Harbor, when Ray Lyman Wilbur, then president of Stanford University, was approached by his young Japanese houseboy.

THAT, TOO, WAS THE WAR

"Sir," said the houseboy, "as you know, Japanese fleet about to arrive in San Francisco Bay on good-will tour. Could I have three days off, to see my countrymen?"

"Certainly," said President Wilbur, "go right ahead."

A couple of days later the educator, along with a group of prominent San Franciscans, was invited to meet the high-ranking officers of the visiting Japanese fleet. As Wilbur was moving along the white-gloved line, shaking hands with admirals, he suddenly came upon the outstretched hand of his houseboy, nattily attired in the uniform of an admiral's aide. Wilbur started to make a surprised comment, then thought better of it, bobbed his head quickly, and walked on.

When the houseboy reported back to work on the Stanford campus, Wilbur said: "Say, that *was* you, wasn't it, in that lineup of admirals?" The houseboy nodded and explained with a perfectly dead pan: "Yes, sir. You see, I am nephew of Admiral Nomura." Sputtered Wilbur: "But I don't understand. Why are you working as my houseboy?"

"Because," said the young Japanese to the distinguished educator and ex-Cabinet member, "my uncle thought it would be good experience for me to work in household of typical middle-class American family!"

San Francisco during the war. Loaded transports filing in out of the Bay, slipping through the Golden Gate in the hush of night. Planeloads of VIP's roaring in stratospherically from the far Pacific and far Washington, jamming the St. Francis and the Mark and the Fairmont and the Palace with

81

big "this is off the record" talk and the clinking of many glasses. The Shore Patrol and the Military Police, walking the dimmed-out streets of the tenderloin two by two, looking unreasonably alert until you notice the blank, faraway looks in their eyes. The busy women of the AWVS, proud and neat in their uniforms, dashing around town in smart station wagons on missions of no less than the utmost importance to the war effort.

(Just after Pearl Harbor a new business was born on Market Street, near the Orpheum Theater. It was called: "Ye Olde Colonial First Aid Shoppe.")

The hectic years. Tin-helmeted war workers, with tin lunch-boxes under their arms, riding to duty on the rattletrap, jam-packed streetcars. Soldiers, looking almost warlike in their plastic helmet liners, roaring up and down the hills in the Army's workhorse six-by-sixes, whistling at the girls in the time-honored, wearying tradition. The every-dawn sight of sleepy-eyed sailors and their "sea gulls" trooping out of the tiny hotels along Eddy and Ellis, the sailors running slightly in their impatience to get back to their ships in time, the girls in an equal hurry to find a bed just to sleep in.

(I remember a conversation I overheard in a Chinatown bar called the Twin Dragons. A sailor slipped onto a stool next to an attractive, unescorted girl, and eventually said to her, blandly enough: "Say, haven't I met you somewhere before?" She studied him for a second and shook her head. "Hm," shrugged the sailor, returning his attention to his drink. "Large world, isn't it?")

THAT, TOO, WAS THE WAR

The hysterical nights. Civilian patriots in saloons, buying drink after drink for supercilious, slightly contemptuous young GI's listening with deaf ears to their self-appointed hosts' recital of their prowess in World War I. The fat black marketeers, comparing notes, nylons, and stacks of gas coupons, dining on finagled filets and getting drunk on smuggled scotch. The unabashed draft dodgers, walking around proudly with deferment cards in their pockets and telling tales of The Man to See and How Much. The lonely, deadpan kids from faraway places like Texas and Georgia, standing on street corners till curfew time and then shuffling back to duty, wordlessly, haplessly.

(One afternoon in the St. Francis I noticed a cabdriver dropping coin after coin into a pay telephone while a young GI talked feverishly into the mouthpiece. After the soldier had hung up and left, the cabby explained: "Aw, the kid was from Tennessee and was darn near crazy with homesickness. Just wanted to talk to his mother. So I got her on the line for him, and then kept feedin' the phone so he could talk to her. He didn't have enough dough, of course." When I started to praise him, the cabby begged off: "Ferget it, ferget it. I always keep a bunch of lead slugs in my back pocket for kids like that.")

The home front in action. Amid all the griping and all the easy cynicism, wonderful women writing letters every day to dozens of servicemen in the overseas theaters. Young war widows, trying to forget, with a riveter's gun in their small hands. Tired, aging men working twice as hard all day and patrolling for Civilian Defense at night. Housewives inventing strange dishes out of unrationed foods and trying to keep themselves from smelling the unmistakable perfume of sizzling steaks cooking in the apartment of the "smart" couple down the hall. The pictures of the war heroes in the bootblack stands and barbershops—MacArthur, Eisenhower, F.D.R., Stilwell . . .

(A couple of horse-loving GI's, assigned to the cavalry and afraid they might be switched momentarily to the tank corps, cornered General "Vinegar Joe" Stilwell at the USO on Market Street one night and got to talking about the value of horses in war. "Say, General," one of them wondered, "didja have any horses over in the China-Burma-India theater?" The general nodded. "And how were they?" persisted the young cavalryman hopefully. "Tasty," answered the general, "mighty tasty.")

The growing signs of victory. Rotation, replacement, discharges, and homemade banners on Richmond District houses reading "Welcome Home, Charlie!" The first United Nations conference at the Opera House, trying to complete its business amid an endless round of cocktail parties (some of the Opera House credentials were signed by a youngish man named Alger Hiss). At last the Japanese surrender, touching off one of the wildest, and in many ways most disgraceful celebrations in a wild city's often disgraceful history. The veterans, still proudly wearing their overseas ribbons and their battle stars, still refreshingly eager to tell where they'd been, what they'd seen, how The Thing Had Been Done.

(This happened one night in 1945 on Powell Street, near

THAT, TOO, WAS THE WAR

California. A Japanese youth approached an elderly mustached man and said: "Pardon me, can you tell me the way to Chinatown?" "What do *you* want to go to Chinatown for?" sneered the other. "You're a Jap!" "Yes," the Nisei smiled, "and *you're* a German!" There was a moment of silence, broken at last by the oldster's surprised "How do you know?" "Because," snapped the Japanese kid, flipping back his overcoat to reveal an honorable-discharge button, "I killed plenty of 'em in Italy.")

The long road back—to normalcy? Not quite. Postwar San Francisco would never be the San Francisco of 1941, any more than the post-fire city could recapture all that perished in 1906. In four years a city that had basked in its own semi-private esteem had come apart at the seams. All of a sudden it was bulging with long-neglected problems that seemed miniscule during a global war, mountainous in the first dawn of peace—problems of transportation and housing and readjustment. The "old" natives realized, with some degree of fright, that 200,000 "outsiders" had discovered San Francisco and its hoarded delights and had decided to stay. What to do with them, where to put them?

(But still, the war was over, and that was the main thing, for a while, at least. It took Mr. and Mrs. Joe Chew of Sausalito to herald the return of peace most simply and naturally. During the war they had two children, whom they had promptly named Winston Franklin Chew and Josef Chew. When their third child was born early in 1946, neighbors eagerly asked what name they'd selected. "Tyrone," reported Mrs. Chew.)

11.

SUDDENLY IT'S SPRING

There's a bright new crinkle to the greenery in Golden Gate Park, here and there a dab of color splashes life across the brown Marin hills, and even the raindrops have a touch of tenderness in them—for spring is here, and yet there is no happiness in the world. In the hearts of too many people it is still winter, and the only warmth is in the heat of blind hate . . .

And yet in Maiden Lane they are getting ready for the traditional welcome to the most joyous of all seasons, and Thursday the daffodils will wave by the thousands and Mayor Robinson will make a little speech filled with brave, fine words. But even in Maiden Lane the hollowness and the emptiness will be felt. Only the daffodils can be blind to the clouds that are gathering, only daffodils can look at them without asking "Why?" . . .

86

SUDDENLY IT'S SPRING

It is not as though faith had left the world forever, for at dawn on Sunday 50,000 climbed to the foot of the cross on Mount Davidson, and most of them knew why they went there. Not because all that was good in the world had died when He died, but because hope still lives in the world today. It was Easter in the Holy Land, too, and the memory of violence and bloodshed was fresh, and those who might have prevented it prayed mightily in their far-off churches . . .

Springtime is the season for children, and in the playgrounds of North Beach and Chinatown and the Western Addition they frolic, and on Sunday they hunted for eggs painted with gay colors. It's great to be a kid in America. So much to live for. But what can kids do about grown men who swagger around with chips of doom on their shoulders? . . .

Saturday was a typical spring day. A lot of people lowered the tops of their convertibles and headed for Bay Meadows, and a lot of other people sat in Seals Stadium with their sleeves rolled up, and cold Cokes sold like hot cakes. Even that sad excuse for an Ocean Beach was filled with people turning their faces to the sun. A little world of people, sitting in the warmth for a breathlessly wonderful moment, with their eyes closed. But even then, and for all their dreams, time was not standing still—and they knew it . . .

Along Post Street and Geary and Grant Avenue spring is not alone a thing of the heart, but of the hat. Atop the heads of the outrageously eternal woman the roses and the tulips and the ribbons bob up and down, and in the St. Francis and El

Prado and the Palace they peer out from under their bonbons and assess each other from the top of their heads to the bottom of their headdresses. Sweet foolishness, the kind that men love; Jan Masaryk liked silly hats on lovely women too . . .

Spring. The goat's head on the brewery truck tells you it's here, in the form of Bock. The tennis players tell you it's here, by wearing shorts instead of long whites. San Francisco pauses at a flower stand to put a blossom in its buttonhole and office managers begin drawing up schedules for summer vacations. What kind of season do you think they'll have—at Lake Success? . . .

Even in San Francisco, where the weather is always the same yet never the same, you know that the days of change are here. Already the nights are shorter, and the morning air is slowly losing its bite. And in the afternoons the old people may sit in Union Square and feel the creeping warmth in their bones. Even the ageless character who putters along the California Street cable slots with an oilcan has a new straw hat. Cable cars and straw hats—can you think of two better symbols of peace? And, some people will say, just as dated . . .

But the good months are ahead, and there are things to be done. Lawns to be cut and houses to be painted. On many a Sunday now the Bay will be bright with white sails, and on the flat rooftops the bodies will start to burn. Market Street will be put together again, and at one end the Ferry Building will look more in need of a spring cleaning than ever, and at the other end Twin Peaks will cover itself with a new carpet. Yes, a lot of little things to be done, in the unspoken hope that the Big Thing will not have to be done . . .

And yet, of all the rites of spring it is still the worship of flowers that is its most typical expression. Flowers in profusion along the outside windows of Macy's. Flowers in bowers behind the glass of the White House's main floor. More perfume than ever from the flower stands, no longer mingling with but now overpowering the smells from the streets . . .

For everywhere it is spring, and in the cemeteries of France and Okinawa and Sicily and Belgium and Iwo Jima the first tender shoots are appearing between the rows of white crosses that still look new.

12.

THE GREAT HORSE OPERA

If there are two events dear to the heart of every stylish San Franciscan—and there are—those two events are the opening of the opera season and the opening of the fall horse-racing season. In 1948, by an utterly utt coincidence, both these forgettable events occurred on the same day.

And quite a day it was, as I recall. Tear gas erupted at Richmond (seems there was an oil strike going on at the time), Harry Bridges' longshoremen picketed Fort Mason to protest something or other, and through it all gaily paraded the town's glitterbug set, putting in a hell of a day too.

In fact, the hours were strictly non-union, with no overtime. For those who work at playing, H-Hour came at 1:30 P.M., when the first race was getting under way on opening day at Golden Gate Fields and the final mopping up wasn't completed until about 4 A.M. the next day at the end of the Opera Ball at the Palace.

THE GREAT HORSE OPERA

Anyway you look at it—even with jaundiced eye—that's about fifteen hours of spending and drinking and eating and listening and saying "Hello, how've you been?" over and over to people who answer "Fine, how've *you* been?" Small wonder that those who followed the rugged route from start to finish wound up as punchy as time clocks, their white ties askew (*Gesundheit*) and their arches flatter than the small talk.

The Day (need I say that it officially launched the autumn social season in San Francisco?) started brightly enough at the handsome Albany horse emporium. Before hardly a single two-dollar bet had been clocked on the tote board, Goldie, the demon maître d'hôtel in the posh Turf Club, was trying to explain to angry patrons why there weren't more tables available, and self-appointed touts were scampering around cajoling suckers into betting on beasts that would have been surprised and flattered to hear such nice things being said about them.

Naturally, this being "The Sport of Kings" (and why is that?), the fairest flower and the thickest cream of San Francisco's business and social world were flowering and curdling all over the Turf Club, some of them even pushing quite rudely in their mad desire to get to the betting windows.

Seen everywhere at once, for instance, was the beauteous Ronnie Waters Thornally, complete with flowers in the hair and a creamy complexion, who just flew in from Hawaii for the opening—"I wouldn't miss it for *anything!*" If flying in from the Islands for the inaugural of a hoss-race jernt seems like undue haste to you, it's because you ain't got the proper feel for things like this. Peasant.

There was also Billy Woodfield, the most Potent 'Tater of the Mystic Shrine, looking quite mystified at a mimeographed sheet of inside tips. And those eminent restaurateurs, Joe Vanessi, Gene Engle, and Trader Vic Bergeron, paying the price of horse meat. Oh yes, and Steelman Bill Gilmore, who owns many a race horse, bending over to whisper sweet somethings into the ear of Tycoon Henry Kaiser.

Mr. Kaiser was later observed walking alone and unashamed up to one of the two-dollar windows—and buying a show ticket. I thought maybe Joe Frazer might like to know that his partner isn't the kind that goes out on a limb, even after a tip from a man who feeds the horses' mouths.

Well, as the sun was sinking slowly in the west (big deal!) the horsy set rushed out to their cars and headed back to town, leaving in their wake a trail of torn ticket stubs. For the day was just beginning as it was ending, and it wasn't destined to end until a new day was beginning, and if there's any other way out of that sentence, I thank you.

Scarcely an hour later these quick-change artists of the *haut monde* (or, as it is pronounced in Scotland, "hoot, mon") were wriggling into their white ties and trailing gowns and scuttling into the St. Francis Mural Room, where Ernest and Bobby, the earnest and bobbing captains, saw to it that everybody was fed fatly in nothing flat. For it's traditional to bolt your food and dash over to the Grand Ole Opry House in plenty of time to see who else is there wearing what with whom. And why?

Naturally, everybody was there as expected, some of them wearing plenty of everything and some of them wearing plenty of nothing, and all of it looking like it cost plenty of something. All I can say is, Merchant Grover Magnin didn't seem displeased, Merchant Jimmy Ransohoff looked cheerful, and Merchants Randolph Hale and Carl Livingston appeared quite urbane. Attorney Bill Wallace yawned.

Countess Gratzos, who is as inevitable at an opera opening as Gaetano Merola (and he *has* to be there), was around with orchids piled inevitably atop her head and her back as bare as a bareback. In the basement bar Bee Goman glittered in a mother-of-pearl jacket, accompanied by her husband, Ray, who blended in nicely with his father-of-pearl cufflinks. And the standout in the Golden Horseshoe lounge was the noted Hollywood historian, Hedda Hopper, wearing lots of pearls and a personality that matched.

All in all, it was a great night for pearls.

After the opera (it was *Falstaff*, and Critic Alfred Frankenstein and I thought it was great even though the patrons applauded as though they were afraid they'd damage their wrist watches) the mob that had started out so bravely twelve hours earlier at the horse races raced over to the Palace for the annual Opera Ball. And still going strong, I might say.

Mrs. Richard Herman of the Junior League surveyed the scene through an honest-to-gosh lorgnette, Garret McEnerney

II towered at least two feet over everybody else, the opera stars took a dutiful bow, and Herbert Richards, who owns the Arthur Murray Dance Studios, couldn't dance because he had a broken toe that he got from kicking a cocktail table, or somebody.

And so the greatest day in the year for many a San Franciscan came to an end. A long, hard day—horse races, operas, balls. The pickets over in Richmond might have had tear gas thrown at them, but the effects of *that* lasted for only a few minutes.

13.

MEMORIAL DAY—1949

You think about things like this today. About the kids who bought a one-way passage to North Africa and Tinian, Normandy and Attu. Especially the kids from San Francisco, because you're back and they're not, you were lucky, they weren't—and who knows why it was like that?

You can't help thinking about the guy from the Sunset who stopped a sniper's bullet at Saint Lo, and the paisano from North Beach who cashed in at Guam, and the boy from Pacific Heights whose last C-47 mission over the Hump ended in a question mark.

You think about them because you knew them and their gripes and their hopes of getting back to San Francisco.

They didn't want much, these kids who grew up in your neighborhood and ended their short lives in black type at the head of a casualty list. On a day like today you can remember

95

the way they used to talk about San Francisco—and that's about all they used to talk about while sweating in the African desert, or freezing in the Ardennes. They just wanted to come back and do the simple things that slowly become the most important things in the world.

There was the B-26 pilot whose home was in the endless avenues of the Richmond. He was a dark, handsome kid with a mustache—and he was generally unhappy. After a mission he'd sit on his bunk in a Nissen hut and talk about his wife: "I was a louse, I guess. Never used to take her out, and I'd gripe my head off every time she bought a hat or a dress. Just between us, I volunteered—to get out of the whole mess. But we've been writing to each other again—and now I can see what a great gal she was. Things are gonna be different when I get back."

He'd pause, flip a cigarette into the butt can, and look far away to a spot between two great bridges.

"Yup. Think we'll get one of those Doelger houses, go to the movies a couple of times a week, and maybe on Saturday nights I'll buy her a corsage and take her dancing to the Mark. She likes junk like that."

On his twenty-second mission, Nazi flak on the French coast got his B-26 and blew it out of the sky.

(I see his widow every once in a while . . . She's going out and around now, of course, and the other night we got to talking about the boy in the B-26 . . . "No," she remembered, "we didn't get along very well, but he was a nice guy.

We wrote some letters back and forth and said a lot of things maybe we meant and maybe we didn't. I'm sorry he was killed. But I don't think we'd ever have made a go of it" . . . She gulped at her drink, there in the Mark lounge on a Saturday night. She was wearing orchids.)

Henry used to call himself a "4-F in uniform," because he was a sort of stylish stout who wore thick glasses and worked in a rear-echelon headquarters in London. "And I'm proud of it," he'd say in a pub just off Fleet Street. "I'm no hero. All I wanna do is get back to the dear old Mission district, the best part of San Francisco, whatta place!" He always said that belligerently, as if he expected you to make something of it.

Whenever London's chilling air-raid sirens would go off to herald the V-1's, Henry would be the first to leave for shelter. "Me, I take no chances," he'd tell you. "I'm getting back to the Mission if I have to become a general's driver. Boy—look at this fog and listen to those sirens! If you don't listen too long, you might think you're back home, hearing the siren on the Ferry Building."

Henry didn't make it to the shelter one night. The V-bomb must have landed right on him, because they couldn't even find his dog tags.

(Henry's family is well-adjusted by this time . . . In their old-fashioned home in the Mission they talk about Henry objectively, like someone they'd known long, long ago . . .

"He was such a nice boy," his mother said, looking lovingly at his picture on the wall. "We miss him so much." She paused, then went on bravely: "Well, I guess we're not the only ones who lost sons" . . . But her eyes weren't quite clear as she stared out at the thick fog . . . It was noon, and in the distance the siren on the Ferry Building began its wail . . . "I've got to go," I said abruptly.)

Al was a sergeant in a cavalry recon outfit—a good-looking, clean-cut kid, like you always see in the recruiting posters. Like most single young GI's from San Francisco (he lived on California Street near Presidio) he was preoccupied with thoughts of food and drink—even in the chill snow of the Ardennes with incoming and outgoing shells waffling around.

"Y'know," he'd say, hopping up and down to keep warm, "I keep thinking about 'em all the time. Those hamburgers they used to have at Vanessi's, I mean. Crunchy ones, full of butter. I can almost feel that butter dribbling down my chin. Sure, I was sloppy, I was. And those sweet ribs over at Vic's. Man! My cavities ache, just thinkin' about 'em." He had a knack of running a gamut of goodies from spot to spot, all over town, till you were drooling along with him.

"See you around a steak at Grison's," was his parting shot as he piled into his jeep and took off. It was days before the Graves and Registration boys from the 35th Division found him deep in the snow, interred by the weather.

(Well, they still have the hamburgers at Vanessi's, but the butter doesn't quite dribble down your chin any more. The postwar world is like that—rough, mighty rough . . . And the steaks are still thick at Grison's, but a little more expensive because of those "conditions," you know—conditions provoked by the war which thoughtfully provided Al with a grave in the snow . . . But Al and his buddies still would have liked the San Francisco they'll never see . . . They'd have liked to laugh at Jerry Lester and try Al Williams' Mexican food and look at Fisherman's Wharf from the big windows at Tarantino's and dance to Eddie Fitzpatrick's music and rediscover Golden Gate Park and the gimmicks out at the Beach . . . It's still pretty much the city they were fighting to get back to, only now it's the city that's going on without them—filled with the steaks they'll never eat and the pretty girls they'll never kiss and the lovely, sunlit days that will live, smile, and die unseen by them . . .)

You think about things like this on Memorial Day—the day when Death gets a holiday.

14.

THE BEST SHOWS IN TOWN

These are some of the things you won't find in the guidebooks
—the sights that San Franciscans look at every day without
seeing:

The gradual rise of a fall dawn out of the East Bay hills,
its pinks and blues as faded as a cheap blanket that has been
washed too many times . . . Cabs, cars, and pedestrians,
scattering leaf-like in the wind at Sutter—as the Powell cable,
cluck-clucking like an old woman with her arms full of bun-
dles, skitters down the hill onto its little cop-made oasis . . .
The ancient characters who sit every day, rain or fog, on the
debris-littered "beach" at Aquatic Park—the "playground
for the people" that turned out to be a cemetery for broken
bottles and dreams to match . . . The painted ladies, the
shifty-eyed "sharp" characters, the bartenders, and the graft-
ers who jam-pack that after-hours Geary St. grocery store

at three in the A.M.—looking as out of place amid the bread, the milk, and the fruit as a neon sign on the Farallones.

The wonderful old-timers who gather every noon at the corner of Seventh and Mission to sift the latest news of the day through their beards; retired cops, saloonkeepers who can remember steam beer for a nickel, pioneers of the Great Fire, seventy-year youngsters who can still read between the lines on one another's faces . . . The Third Street bridge at midnight, its great counterbalance turning it into a hunchback among spans, looking in the dramatic half-light of a street lamp like a stage set for something by Eugene O'Neill or Saroyan . . . The downtown office workers who worry at their desks all day about the exercise they're not getting —and then, at 5 P.M., sprint desperately down the middle of Market to catch a streetcar that's pulling away, threading in and out between cars and pedestrians with all the swivel-hippiness of a Mae West . . . The mysterious, tall jars in the windows of Chinatown's herbalists, filled with cloudy-looking question marks that make your eyebrows raise to your hairline; propped up in front of them, non-informative placards in which you can make out just enough words to confuse you further—like, in Ng Gar Yeun on Clay, "Seals" and "glands" (no puppy-dog's tails?).

The anxious-to-impressive women who sneak into the St. Francis through the Geary and Post entrances and then sweep out grandly under the Powell marquee—so they can join the crowd waiting for the doorman and cab starter to whistle them up a taxi; and the only thing they tip—is the fact that they're phony . . . The corner table in John's Grill, where Cloak 'n' Suiter Morris Goldman, who talks in rhymes and riddles, presides over a table that is hemmed in by such'ns as Lefty O'Doul, Inspector Joe Farrell, Tom Laird, and Babe Herman; every day, a ferocious chew-and-chat fest, where it's not only polite to talk with your mouth full, it's imperative if you want to get a morsel in edgewise . . . The rush-hour crush at the Bay Bridge Terminal—where the commuters, as punchy as their tickets, are heckled daily by a newsboy who shouts: "Huddy, huddy, huddy—only a few trains left!"

The tower of babble rising out of the children's playground at the zoo, loaded to the screaming point with kiddies letting their animal spirits escape from their cages . . . The noon-time parade of politicos in the Palace's Palm Court, their fangs bared in polite smirks as they shake one another's paws and nod as halfably as a woman who has just seen her best new hat on her worst old enemy's head . . . The hysterical between-the-activity at the Geary and Curran, where the play-goers fan out for a recess in the Geary Cellar, or the Show Club, or the Theater Club—till the warning bell summons them to leave their glasses and get back to their classes . . . The Market Street wisenheimers, obvious importations from New York's Broadway and Chicago's Randolph, standing with their low foreheads together and missing nothing that walks by—especially if it has a trim ankle; if we ever have to get rid of the cable cars, I hope these herkimer-jerkimers go along for the ride.

The mystery-mastery of the strong-armed gents who whip

their immense delivery trucks through the Post Street traffic rushes; how they keep from creasing your fenders as they cut in and out is something to make you wrinkle your brow . . . The Sunday softball games on the Potrero playground, fought to a furious finish by eighteen tough, gum-chewing guys who, to your never-ending surprise, turn out to be gals who've got more muscles in their little finger than I've got in my whole head . . . The cigar-chomping characters at Bennie Ford's Monday-night fights, filling the air with blue smoke and oaths to match as they watch the not-so-gladiators maul each other; to these gents of the ringside show those aren't two men fighting under the hot lights—they're merely animate objects to be bet on (at the proper odds, of course); and oddly enough, when the better man wins, sometimes the bettor man loses.

In the middle of a rainstorm automobiles losing their grip on the Powell Street hill and wallowing around frantically and helplessly, like ungainly puppies on a hardwood floor . . . The sea gulls, the swans, the ducks, and the sparrows that frolic in feathery flurries all around the quiet lake in front of the Palace of Fine Arts, their mingled cackles and chirps echoing hollowly through the broken pillars and cracked columns . . . The unfailing thrill of seeing San Francisco with its most beautiful flank exposed as you come out of the darkness of the Waldo Tunnel and float down toward the Gate Bridge—a sight you can look at over and over but never quite get over.

These are some of the things that add up to the best shows in town—and your eyes have it.

15.

THE FULLER LIFE,

San Francisco's eating places are world famous, and justly
so, but sometimes now the food is a little hard to swallow and
sometimes you catch yourself looking up from your table and
staring into empty spaces far across the sea. For famine,
gaunt-eyed and hollow-cheeked, is on a silent rampage, more
deadly and real than the atom bomb . . .

And the atmosphere is quiet and subdued in El Prado too.
Walter, the headwaiter, is sleek and he guides you carefully
to your booth. The cushions are soft, the lights are soft, the
tablecloths white and gleaming. A cocktail first, perhaps? Let
me suggest the canapés—delicious! Or, perhaps m'sieu and
madame prefer antipasto, our own recipe. The filets? But of
course, they're like butter tonight. And a mixed green salad
with croutons—right. Incidentally, we have a wonderful red
Cabernet—you should try it. Oh, before I forget, you *do* like

vichyssoise, don't you? Fine, fine. And for dessert, our Petite Coeur à la Crème, certainly. Thank you.

(In Greece the children die before they ever hear of Homer or the Acropolis, but first the skin becomes taut against their bones and their bellies swell like soccer balls . . .)

And at Seals Stadium the huge crowd roars with amusement as a tiny Negro boy trudges up the stairs, one hot dog disappearing down his throat, two others clutched and poised in his little hands. And at the Beach sunshine and salt spray fill the air and the kids sniff delightedly as they wait for their hamburgers "with everything"; and inside the counters are jammed with the holiday mob toying with meat pies—and "Hey, Joe, try one of them apricot turnovers à la mode, they're strictly moidah." The waitresses are hot and tired and their faces look drawn as they try to keep up with the Sunday demand.

(In Italy the dream of *Fascismo* has long ago withered into a nightmare, and the beggars of a bankrupt empire cry piteously outside every tourist hotel . . .)

The smell of frying food makes your nose prick up its ears every time you near Columbus Avenue and Broadway. Here, the hamburgers are the most extravagant and expensive in town—huge slabs of brown meat between halves of French bread too large to bite comfortably. The waiters stand before great bowls of lettuce and beets and tomatoes, sloshing vinegar and oil with a free hand. But the chefs are the stars of this show, and they know it. In their white uniforms, with towels knotted rakishly around their necks, they putter incessantly

—tossing the spaghetti high and never losing a strand, deftly flipping the thick steak on the charcoal, lighting the brandy on the fried cream so the blue flames rise in the air.

(Millions are doomed in Hunan Province, for even the wild roots and the leaves cannot last forever, and there is no nourishment in mud and clay . . .)

It's fun to dine in Chinatown with James Wong Howe, the movie cameraman, because he knows his way around and he knows what to order. None of the tourist favorites for him. He leads you down a side street and into an out-of-the-way restaurant where the surroundings are starkly functional—just a few tables and chairs, no tablecloths. And the lights are bare and glaring. But no matter. He has a consultation in Chinese with the waiter, and soon the feast appears. Great, golden prawns, fried to a crackling turn. A wondrous combination of beef and cooked walnuts. A strange, gelatinous substance, dead white but flatly attractive to the palate. Sweet and sour pork, with the chunks of pineapple basking in a brown goo. And of course ng ka py, the colorless Chinese drink with the kick of a thousand mules. All this and more, so that when you leave, the serving plates are still half full and the exotic sauces are turning cold and sticky. To be thrown away.

(The average Englishman won't complain too bitterly as long as the stale, foamless beer keeps pouring from the tap in his favorite pub, but maybe that will be cut and there will be less bread and only one egg a week . . .)

Adolph, the headwaiter in the Palace Garden Court, thinks

106

that Eggs Benedict might be nice for a late breakfast. And they are. Two eggs poached and cradled neatly on slices of ham aboard two toasted biscuits. With a lovely yellowish Hollandaise sauce spread lavishly across the top; and of course the chef throws in a few mushrooms for effect. The Englishman across from you hasn't been home since before the war, so now he's accustomed to our beer. He orders another, and toys daintily with hearts of artichoke filled with diced white chicken. He's going home for a visit in about thirty days. He supposes he'll find the old place changed a good bit, what?

(Calories used to be the things a dieting woman talked about in a loud and knowing voice, but now they're the common denominator and Americans are told that they eat 3200 calories a day while in India fifty-five million are existing on less than 960 . . .)

In Rene's on Sacramento Street Jack Earle, the 8 foot 6 inch giant, has just finished cooking a special meal for his friends, and he stalks out of the kitchen to attend personally to your dessert—champagne poured inches deep over great red strawberries. In Omar Khayyam's Restaurant the patrons nibble daintily at huge slabs of unleavened bread, and at the Papagayo tortillas sit in napkins at your elbow and grow cold and die untouched, and in the Mural Room Bobby Nielsen sings the praises of Chicken Tetrazzini, and across the Bay Trader Vic unveils a Hawaiian steak three inches thick and barbecued in soy sauce.

(A former President with a high collar reports that only

107

"if every source of supply is scraped to the bottom of the barrel, we can pull the world through this most dangerous crisis," and in the alleys behind the restaurants of San Francisco the cats prowl by moonlight and grow fat . . .)

16.

SNAPSHOTS OF SAN FRANCISCANS

The drama critics have yet to discover this man in costume. A past master of the art of pantomime, thousands are enthralled by his performances nightly. Part of his effectiveness, I suppose, is owing to the skillful manner in which his act is staged. Surrounded by blackness, he performs under a single powerful spotlight that displays his complete authority. The stark simplicity of his somber attire is relieved only by a single gleaming ornament. His nightly act never fails to win my applause—for he not only stops the show, he stops the traffic . . . The rush-hour traffic cop under the light at Hyde and California.

This gentleman lives atop Nob Hill in solitary splendor. His show-place home is small, even dainty—yet typically San Franciscan with its huge windows opening on the vista of plunging California Street, the grand canyon of Powell, the surrounding castles floating their neon pennants. His is a sedentary, philosophic life, filled with long hours of just sitting and staring at the bright lights and the constant dizzy swirl of people rushing to and fro. He is a man closely tied to one of the richest traditions of Baghdad-by-the-Bay. In fact, he has often said that he doesn't know quite what he will do—when the day and night of the cable car are ended . . . The signalman in the tiny green house at the corner of Powell and California.

Here's a character you've seen in many a movie, and he still moves around with the dash and the swagger that distinguish the thespian. When he talks fondly of his friend "Jimmy," you can bet he means Cagney, and the actor you call Raft is just plain "Georgie" to him. He knows them, and others well, for he was raised with them and played in their pictures. Now he's "retired" from flicker life, although with his wooden leg and his jaunty upcurling mustache, and gold earrings he sometimes wears, he could still do big things in Hollywood. But he's satisfied with his present lot, satisfied to be "The Pirate of the Mission" . . . Joe Costello, who peddles papers at the corner of Seventh and Mission.

His accent marks him as a Britisher, his gait sets him apart as a horseman. And so you're not surprised to learn, upon chatting with him in the wild open spaces near the Beach, that at one time he was a member of a crack British regiment—

110

mounted, of course. He runs a hand through his graying hair as he softly recalls days of glory under the Crown in India, hard sessions on the polo field, equally hard sessions afterward with gin and tonic, or perhaps Pimm's No. 5. Definitely a pukka sahib, Kiplingesque. But the sun is setting on this son of the Empire. His days in the saddle are almost over. And yet, at least he can spend his days near the horses he loves, watching the youngsters trying their skill at the reins . . . Jimmy—the man who operates the kiddies' merry-go-round at the San Francisco Zoo.

She's blond and pretty, this girl with the upturned nose and the down-draft curls. There's hardly a person in the midtown sector that doesn't know her well, for she covers more ground than Golden Gate Park. But although her autograph is one of the most famous in town, I wouldn't say she's popular, exactly. And although she does her job with almost painful efficiency, you could not say that her employers are pleased with her. Maybe it's the way she dresses. You see, she wears slacks—but even so her pink slip is always showing . . . Amy Sliger, the downtown traffic copperette on the tricycle.

He's tall, dark, and handsome, every inch a gentleman of good taste and culture. On Grant Avenue in the heart of the elite shopping district you often see him nodding to the most elegant ladies, who favor him with their prettiest smiles. I can't remember an important social function of the past decade that has not been graced with his presence. An imposing figure, straight as an arrow in his beautifully tailored uniform, he adds the final touch of class to any event. The richest men in town call him by his first name—Joe . . . Joe "Shreve" Foreman, the Negro doorman at Shreve's.

An undying love of the sea lives on in the heart of this ancient mariner. Too old now to take his turn on the bridge, he likes to teeter slowly back and forth in his rocker, take a fresh grip on his pipe, and recall his stormy days and nights as a skipper. With his blue eyes snapping, he spins long tales of great waves that broke over his decks, of the bow of his ship disappearing time and again into the boiling waters, of fogs thicker than any fog before or since. The ex-master of a tramp steamer on the China coast run? . . . No; a captain who spent all his active years on the San Francisco-Oakland ferry run.

His address is one of the fanciest on Nob Hill—and passersby usually look at him with half-envy as he gets out of his car, strolls in under the big canvas awning, and heads for the elevators. With easy familiarity he returns the lobby greetings of the wealthy San Franciscans who are his neighbors—and as the elevator doors close on him, you hear his crisp order: "The penthouse, please." Soon he is relaxed in his glass aerie, where, as he gazes out over the finest unobstructed view in San Francisco, he casually selects phonograph records and listens to their perfect reproduction on his expensive equipment . . . The blond young man who oper-

112

ates the Frequency Modulation radio transmitter on top of the Clay-Jones apartments.

There's a touch of Texas in her voice, a Southern sway to her hips, a certain magnetism that makes men draw closer to her. In the bright-light district, where even powerful men such as Fuller get the brush, she's an undisputed queen. No matter how many people are waiting, a cozy table for two is reserved for her. The drinks are weak, I must admit, but it's nice being with her, and she has the siren knack of making you think she likes being with you. But under her veneer of polish you still know the truth, as hard to shake off as a hangnail: she's only after your money. And although she holds your hand and occasionally raps you around your little finger, let's face it— she works in a clip joint . . . Stevie Stephens, the manicurist at the St. Francis barbershop.

17.

THERE'LL ALWAYS BE A CABLE CAR

I know, you've heard it all before.

Those colorful, picturesque, utterly adorable little cable cars.

Running up and down the impossible hills, filled with ding-dings and cluck-clucks and brave passengers clinging precariously to the outside steps, to each other, to anything, and sometimes nothing. Sentimental curios, riveted to the heart of every San Franciscan with strands of steel. Noisy, illogical, quaint, outmoded, hard to operate, harder yet to maintain, getting in everybody's way while getting somewhere in the slowest possible fashion.

The green Powell Street line and the red California Street line—photographed so often by delighted tourists that they seem almost to yawn as they waddle past the lenses. Breaking down crankily and stupidly in the middle of the heaviest traffic crushes, sitting in the middle of the street and listing slightly to one side in a smug attitude that plainly says: "Don't try to make us hurry. You know and we know that you can't get along without us." Jolting, shoving, jerking along the narrow streets, carrying the past heavily on their shoulders and the present as uncomfortably as possible.

But don't get me wrong. I love the cable cars. What other mode of public transportation brings smiles to the faces of the people who have to ride them? (Even though the smiles are sometimes a little pained and strained.) What other type of municipal conveyance is babied along like a rich old aunt, and tolerated overlong in a job that calls for brisk efficiency instead of gingerbread sentimentality? Only the cable cars of San Francisco—for a variety of reasons, some of them practical, some of them neurotic.

As a tourist attraction, the cables are the greatest thing that has happened to San Francisco since the Chinese decided they liked the local climate. They help make the city look "different," an adjective that would prove a lot less simple to apply without them. And as a way of getting people to and fro (forward motion not always guaranteed) they still do a pretty fair job.

But mainly it is a city's abject sentimentality that gets all fouled up in the cable lines. The citizens want the "dinkies" around as a constant working reminder of a supposedly glorious past that keeps fading away, elusive as fog. As R. L. Duffus once put it, today's San Franciscans know there was some special magic about yesterday's city, but they're no longer sure what it was, or where it was. However, they think the cable cars had something to do with it, and so they insist on seeing them toddling around the streets as long as possible —even to the point of impossibility.

There has always been humor connected with the slightly comical cable cars. Back in the 1880s the whole town giggled about the Chinese cook named Ching Pon, who, upon seeing a Washington Street cable stalled at Polk, hurried over to the gripman and inquired: "Whatsa malla—sling bloke?" For a couple of decades after delighted San Franciscans hurled that pidgin sentence whenever they spotted a cable car stalled in its tracks.

The children of that pre-automobile age had fun with the clacking cables too. A favorite sport of the roller-skating set was to drop a bent wire through the slot, hook onto the strand, and get themselves a free pull up a hill. Other inventive moppets conceived the fanciful idea of hitching empty boxes on a string and snagging them to the cable. It was no uncommon sight to see as many as thirty cartons galloping bravely over a hilltop, while the young gagsters stood cheering and yelling at the bottom.

And the gripmen, apparently, have always been as unique as their vehicles. Obligingly, they'd stop in the middle of a block to let a steady customer dismount directly in front of his home—a courtesy that was usually amply repaid. At Christmastime in the must-have-been-Gay Nineties, every gripman from the California Cable Company would line up at Braunschweiger's Whiskey House to get a gift bottle of rock and rye, as thanks for stopping daily in front of the Braun-schweiger mansion at 2216 California Street.

Today's gripmen do their best to continue the colorful tra-ditions. Once out of the traffic crush, they'll occasionally let an old-time passenger off in front of his door. But they have most of their fun with street names. For instance, there's a Negro gripman on the Powell Street line who gets an oc-casional gift carton of Lucky Strikes for singing out "Ellis— MFT!" as he approaches that intersection. And a California cable conductor steadfastly shouts "Paul Jones" (at Jones) and "Old Taylor" (at the next street), even though he has yet to be rewarded for his commercials.

I saw my favorite cable-car sight one day in 1946, at the corner of Powell and Jackson streets. As the car approached the rugged, right-angle turn there, the conductor leaned out and hollered the traditional "Hang on! 'Kout for the curve!" Then *he* fell off.

Incidentally, I believe I am the only San Franciscan who has ever been bitten by a cable car—and at that very same in-tersection. The story is short and painful. I was sitting in one of the slatted outside seats on a particularly loose-in-the-joints Powell car, and as it creaked around the curve—well, all I can say is that I was bitten, and I still have a small scar to prove it. I plan to leave this private blemish to the Smith-sonian Institution, where, I hope, it will be displayed over a sign reading "San Francisco Cable Scar."

Of course practically every San Franciscan has his own gag about the cables. For instance, if you're a tourist, don't walk up to a San Franscynic and ask him how the cars operate. A favorite, bored retort is: "Well, you see that gimmick there in the middle? It's got a gizmo on the end that hooks onto the dingbat in the slot—that's all there is to it."

Another phenomenon of the cable car is that you generally see two or three pedestrians running after one, and for a very good reason. The cars seem never to stop in the same place twice. Sometimes they halt at the traditional corner, but if there are automobiles in the way, or they have an intersecting cable line to cross, they'll come to rest on the next corner, without signal, without explanation. John Wright, a seasoned observer of the local scene, recently defined a San Franciscan as "a person who can predict where a cable car is going to stop."

However, sometimes even the operators aren't sure. On California Street last year my friend Leah Siewert saw a cable car arrive at Franklin Street three times in one trip. The jam-packed car started up the hill from Van Ness Avenue, and just as the conductor yelled "Franklin!" it went into a slip and slid back to the bottom. Taking a deep breath, the cable started up again. The conductor called out "Franklin again!" And once more it lost its grip at the crest of the hill. This time the passengers on the steps dismounted and walked along-side as the crate slowly got to the top, whereupon the conductor groaned loudly: "For the third and last time—Franklin!"

THERE'LL ALWAYS BE A CABLE CAR

Nevertheless, those who know the cable cars best love 'em the most. A Powell Street conductor one day explained to me why he's so crazy about the rickety ground grippers. "Look," he said. "I'm standing on the back platform, and my cap falls off. So do I get excited? Do I signal for a halt? Nyah. I jump off, pick up my cap, run back, and jump on again. What other kind of transportation moves so slow and easy-like these days?"

Another conductor I know is in the habit of jumping off his cable as it trundles past the Dunkit Donut Shop on Columbus Avenue near Chestnut. He runs inside, yells "Gimme six!" grabs the bag of doughnuts and catches up with his still-moving car without even a sprint. A third conductor holds up three fingers as he passes Bruno's Lunchroom at Columbus and Taylor, which is the signal for Bruno to get three hamburgers ready. Then, on the cable's return trip from the Bay-Taylor turntable, the conductor dashes in, picks up his 'burgers, and gallops back to his car.

But any discussion of the cable cars must return inevitably to the tourist aspect. They still fascinate the outsider. Even so seasoned a traveler as Phil Baker, the radio comedian, was incensed at the recent hullabaloo over abandoning the lines in favor of busses. "Why," he said indignantly, "San Francisco without its cable cars would be like a kid without his yo-yo."

The best description I've encountered of the typical tourist reaction was contained in a memo written recently by an employee of a large San Francisco firm to his boss, to explain why he was late to work one day. It went like this:

DEAR BOSS: I was late to work this morning. Why?

Boarded Washington–Jackson cable at Fillmore. Man, wife, eight-year-old boy, and a young couple—all tourists—aboard. At Webster, gripman stopped car so the father could walk ahead and take movies of his wife and kid as the car passed. Stopped again, of course, so Father could board car again. When gripman stopped to let Mother off to take pictures of Dad and kid, I offered to take the movies, figuring if I got the whole group in at once, we'd get along on time. I got the pictures.

But when we reached the top of the hill (by Lafayette Park) the gripman pointed out Alcatraz. That did it. We stopped at each of the next two intersections for movies of the Bay view and the Rock.

Meanwhile, the gripman was playing with the boy, who was much more interested in the cable car than the view. Kid would shout "ding da-ding ding," and the gripman would add the last two bongs on the car's bell.

We stopped again at the carbarn on Mason, where a pair of overalled workmen appeared with a grip to replace the one on our car. The tourists, as expected, stayed aboard to watch the transfer. I and a few other San Franciscans boarded a passing Bay–Taylor cable after our conductor shouted to the other that it was okay, we all had paid our fares.

Anyway, boss, that's why I was late to work this morning. But one thing I'm sure of. That pixie cable-car crew made friends for San Francisco—and gave those tourists the high spot of their vacation.

In fairness to the anti-cable car contingent, though, I suppose I should note that an occasional visitor experiences that letdown feeling. For instance, Mrs. Stewart Brown recently entertained as her house guest an Eastern woman who had never before visited San Francisco; so the first thing she wanted to do, of course, was see the cables. Mrs. Brown walked her over to California Street, where the visitor watched for a few minutes, then shrugged and sighed in a deeply disappointed tone:

"Let's go home. I thought they were *suspended* from cables!"

18.

THE RISE OF FALL

If there's one thing San Francisco is famous for, besides its scenery, it's the weather. "Never too cool—never too hot." That's the line you get on a barrage basis from the Chamber of Commerce, and that's the line echoed all over the world by ex-San Franciscans longing for the crispness of the Bay atmosphere.

In fact, the only people who seem to have any kicks about the weather are the deep-dyed Easterners. They sometimes claim they miss the first gleaming snowfall of winter and the dripping excitement of the early spring thaw. Intense summer heat? And midwinter slush? Well, let's not talk about *that*.

As for me, I'd like to argue the old assumption that San Francisco is "the city of no seasons." It's true, part of the time, that you can't tell winter from summer, and that you're liable to freeze in July and get a sunburn playing tennis in January. But if that isn't Autumn—with a capital *A*—that I feel in October, then the chill in my bones just means that, darling, I am growing older and colder. And if all the sights and sounds of Baghdad-by-the-Bay at that time don't indicate a very definite season of the year, you may bottle me up in the Stockton Tunnel and use Coit Tower as a stopper.

You can see autumn in the late, cold light of dawn, when the new day throws an icy greeting across the Bay. Only it isn't the crisp newness of a summer morning; a fall day looks like it's been used.

There is a gray cast to the sun's gold, and you can blow out your breath and see goose pimples on it. The air, colder than a B-girl's heart, takes a nip at you, and your nose turns the color of a stoplight. You snuggle into your overcoat collar and agree that it's cool in San Francisco; cool—a four-letter synonym for cold in San Francisco.

This is autumn all right. As the sun fights through to score a few points, the atmosphere becomes sharp and clear—and you can tell it's fall by the spring that suddenly appears in everyone's steps. You take a deep nosegay of melted icicles, as bracing as chilled champagne, and decide to pass up the cable car for a walk to work. In the crystal morning air along Market, far-off Twin Peaks suddenly loom close and brown, as though they were a block away, and you can see the crawling things that are automobiles moving blackly across the Bridge. The sky takes on the thin, pale blue of the typical autumn day—as typical in New Haven as it is here.

Now the ladies are parading on Post Street and Grant Avenue and now the fur coats are worn not for appearances alone. And the cops in their blue jackets blow on their hands as well as their whistles—and think back to the summer days when they directed traffic in their shirt sleeves and the warmth shrank San Francisco into a small town. No longer can the office workers get a quick noontime suntan on the lawn of Union Square—the poor man's Palm Springs; now they sit on the benches with their hands in their pockets and stare contemplatingly at their outstretched feet. The faces are whiter, for this is autumn in the city that knows no seasons.

The bartenders, who mix a city's tempo as well as its drinks, can tell you what time of year it is. The day of the cooling Tom Collins has disappeared into the early evening of warming whisky. The cocktail hour no longer starts at 2 P.M. with a thirst for gin—it gets under way more normally at 5 P.M. with the customers striding in briskly, flipping their overcoats onto a hook, and calling, with many a dramatic "brrr," for an old-fashioned. Already there are requests for Tom and Jerry, those two alcoholic gentlemen whose spirits rise as the temperature drops.

Gone are the golden days from Golden Gate Park, and in the once sun-sweetened corners the shrubs tremble as though in need of an extra blanket. And the grassy lawns, where picnicking families gathered nightly just a few weeks ago, lay bare and barely green. At the Beach the waves pound more heavily, and the little white horses of the surf leap about to keep warm. But still there are the hardy ones who refuse to say farewell to summer, standing bravely on the cold sand in their shorts and wading into the water that is ten degrees colder than cold. Even the sea lions, huddled together on the rocks, seem to be discussing their foolhardihood.

Autumn is the social season, too, and there's a cocktail party every hour on the hour. Where do you want to go? The list is endless, the thirst is boundless, the glasses are bottomless—and you can find your Lost Weekend in any of a dozen smart drawing rooms. Always the same talk, the same cigarettes smoldering in the ash trays, the same tiny burns on the hardwood floors.

No, it doesn't take burning leaves and anti-freeze to tell you that this is the downfall of the year. Already the department stores are signing up their Santa Clauses, and now the Skid Rowgues tag you for a quarter to find "a warm place to sleep tonight." Wool mufflers are the latest style note on the necks of the cable-car gripmen, and on Powell Street the legless beggars put newspapers between themselves and the cold sidewalk and are too busy rubbing their thin arms to hold out their hats to your hearts. The gay small talk is of football and coming ski trips, not of baseball and Tahoe.

And so autumn comes to the city of no seasons. The days are short, and no twilight falls, only the sudden curtain of night, illuminated almost immediately by the neon that stands out sharply in the crisp air. The fog that creeps in is different too—dirtier, grayer, colder. Yet there is no gloom in the long nights that lay ahead for Mr. and Mrs. San Francisco— and there is always magic in Baghdad-by-the-Bay. Who knows? Tomorrow may be the hottest day of the year!

19.

THAT WAS SAN FRANCISCO

Even veteran world travelers, well-seasoned in their salt-and-pepper tweeds, seem to agree that it was quite a town in the olden, golden days. "The greatest city I ever visited," one global gadabout once told me, "was San Francisco—a city that died in 1906."

That, of course, is the rather annoying attitude of the super-sentimentalist, who looks at yesterday with longing and at to-day with disdain. For "old" San Francisco still lives, in out-of-the-way corners, in endless conversations among today's graybeards, in the musty attics of many a memory. Today, it is a city that continues to grow—chained always to the past —a past that is ever present.

Old San Francisco. "The city that was never a small town" definitely had something, and whatever it was, they still talk about it. Not in the manner of the historians, with meaningless dates and esoteric anecdotes, but in an endless mumble-

jumble of names and places and happenings that still seem
tinged with a special kind of brightness.

"Do you remember?" the old-timer always demands. Yes,
remember:

When a jockey named "Snapper" Garrison rode the great
horse Boundless to an amazing victory in the Ninety-three
Fair—giving birth to the term "Garrison finish." When a
gang of pioneer ruffians used to shout "huddle 'em, huddle
'em!" as they crowded around their victims—thus coining
the word "hoodlum." When a gambler who hung around the
Cliff House used to challenge his fellow bettors in a loud
phrase that he invented to live forever: "All right, put up or
shut up!"

Remember the old Orpheum on O'Farrell Street? Its
regular customers held their regular seats for the gala Sun-
day-night performances year after year—and the great ambition of every prominent San Franciscan was to get a permanent pass to the theater. So one day Charles L. Ackerman,
president of the Orpheum, bestowed this most princely of
favors upon Horace Platt, president of the now also defunct
Geary Street Railway. Platt was overjoyed until he noticed,
in small letters at the bottom of the pass, the following legend:
"Not good on Saturdays, Sundays, or holidays."

So he had a special Geary Street Railway pass made for
Ackerman. On the bottom of the card was printed, in equally
small letters: "Not good going east or west"—the only directions traveled by his company.

The old Orpheum. A lot of tears have been shed over it.

When he appeared for the last time on its stage, Ted Lewis had to pull his old silk hat down over his eyes—to hide his grief. Today, there is nothing to mark its site. Where a generation of San Franciscans enjoyed the greatest performers of the age only a parking lot stands, or sits. Perhaps the last San Franciscan to "enjoy" the Orpheum was a real estate operator named Maurice Moskovitz. Just before the wreckers went to work, he sneaked inside, found his old "permanent" chair, and sat there alone for a few minutes. Yes. He cried too.

The City That Was. Remember when all the horsecars were converted to cables—sometime in the Nineties, wasn't it?—and hundreds of homeless families flocked to buy the suddenly outmoded conveyances? These they hauled out to the sand dunes near Ocean Beach to convert into homes, and overnight the "city" of Carville was born.

For years the horsecarmmunity flourished. Potted geraniums flowered in the streetcar windows, and the wealthier squatters blossomed out with lace curtains. Where the well-to-do of today sport two automobiles, the aristocrats of Carville owned two horsecars, tacked together to form a single dwelling.

But Carville was doomed around 1910, when the city decided to grade the Great Highway that runs grandly along the ocean front. The horsecar forerunner of the Sunset District was condemned, and the squatters sadly gathered their pitiful baggage and trooped desolately across the sands in a new pilgrimage to poverty.

But San Francisco had an especially gala Fourth-of-July celebration that year. As massed thousands watched from the surrounding dunes, the Fire Department destroyed Carville in a blaze that still burns in the memories of oldsters. Trumpeted the mayor as the embers glowed to death: "May San Franciscans never again be reduced to living under such miserable conditions."

(Brave words those. But today many a San Franciscan, living in an unlighted basement, would welcome a horsecar to call home . . .)

The old days. Once you start dreaming, the recollections come flittering back in clusters.

Those Sunday mornings in the Ferryboat Era, when you met your friends under the Ferry Building's clock, and flipped coins to decide which ride to take. If you felt like a long trip, there were the *Gold* and the *Petaluma,* which made the thirty-eight-mile run to Petaluma in six or eight hours, depending on how long you had to wait for the Black Point Bridge to open. Or you had your choice of the Monticello Steamship Company's *Ashbury Park* and *General Frisbee,* waiting to take you in elegant style to Vallejo.

At Pier 3 you might pause for a look at the *J. D. Peters* and the *Port of Stockton,* or nearby the *Delta King* or *Delta Queen,* on the memorable Sacramento River run. (Ah, those moonlit prohibition nights along the Sacramento, with one of the big *Deltas* majestically rounding a bend, her white wake dotted with empty bottles bobbing up and down in an endless string!)

But usually, after you counted your small change, you compromised on the best nickel ride in the world—on the Creek Route's *Encinal* or *Thorofare*, fifty minutes from the south end of the Ferry Building to First and Broadway in Oakland, with good meals and plenty of time to eat them.

The vanished ferryboats. For long, slow-moving decades they seemed rooted permanently to the Bay, like mobile counterparts of Goat Island and Angel Island and Alcatraz. There was much talk of bridges, but such miracles seemed centuries away. Surely there would always be the ferries, the white ones and the orange ones, hauling sleepy-eyed commuters in the morning and tired-eyed commuters in the evening, bleating around in the fog at half-speed and only occasionally nudging into the steel wall of a tanker, lugging knicker-clad hikers to Marin County every Sunday for a hike up Tamalpais, lazing around on moonlit nights in the blessed pre-jukebox days as a three-piece orchestra played dreamy Viennese waltzes and young couples sat staring into space on the deck with their fingers tightly interlocked.

Old San Francisco. So much to remember.

Jack Johnson, the great fighter, training at the Beach, and the mobs that gathered, at fifty cents a head, to watch him work out on a punching bag. At the end of the session he'd unlease his mighty muscles and knock the bag off its moorings and into the crowd—finders keepers.

Rosetta Duncan, later to become famous playing "Topsy" to her sister Vivian's "Eva," doing a little Dutch-boy act at

John Tait's O'Farrell Street café—and quitting when he refused a five-dollar-a-week raise. The late great movie comedian, "Fatty" Arbuckle, showing that he had a heart somewhere in his heft by buying new mattresses for every prisoner in the county jail. Jack Warner, now one of Hollywood's powerful Warner Brothers, running a tiny theater on Fillmore Street near Sutter—and having the nightly receipts changed into nickels so he could count them out with his now-forgotten partner ("one for you, one for me"). The pretty little usherette at the Castro Theater, whose name meant nothing then; a few years later every movie-goer was talking about Janet Gaynor.

The memorable night when Tessie Wall, the madame, shot her estranged husband, Frankie Daroux, in Anna Lane—then calmly awaited arrest and later offered to save his life by donating her blood. The great fighter, Stanley Ketchel, showing up at Shreve's swank jewelry store on the morning after a successful fight, wearing a dressing gown and escorting a beautiful woman for whom he'd casually select expensive trinkets. "Dasher Jack" Cannon, the Beau Brummell of the Police Department, who always carried an ultra-thin, silver-plated gun, a gift from a visiting celebrity named Rudolf Valentino, who was impressed with the officer's impeccable clothes and insisted that the ordinary service revolver caused an unsightly bulge.

The names, the faces, the places that stick in your mind! Charlie Chaplin, Gentleman Jim Corbett, and the Great Fitzsimmons, giving free shows every Sunday at the Chutes on

Haight Street. The block bounded by Powell, Ellis, Mason, and Eddy, containing more nationally known cafés than any other block in the country—the Louvre with its imported beers, the Oriental, Teddy Lundstet's, Shiff & Dow's, the Langam, Pratt & Tierney's, Spider Kelly's, Jack Morgan's, the Inverness, Haymarket, and the original Techau Tavern. Louis Coutard, the chef at the old Poodle Dog, proudly concocting the delicacy that still bears his name—Crab Louis.

The celebrated sea lion, Ben Butler, that used to sit in front of the Cliff House and patiently shake flippers with thousands of local yokels each Sunday. And the two trained canaries that were the cutest sight to see at Sutro Baths (one of the birds would pull the lanyard of a tiny cannon, whereupon the other one would fall "dead" into a miniature coffin). The great sensation of 1910: Jim Woods, manager of Hotel St. Francis, making the public pronouncement that henceforth women would be allowed to smoke in the lobby and hallways. And creating no sensation at the 1915 Fair—a young, curly-haired man playing the piano in front of Sid Grauman's Chinese concession; today you know him as Harry Richman.

Colorful characters, colorful customs, colorful costumes.

That favorite South o' Market celebrity, "Uncle Sam," the candy man, dressed to the hilt in top hat, starred coat, and striped pants: in one hand he carried a bunch of toy balloons that "cried" as the air slowly escaped from them, and in the other he clutched an ugly blacksnake whip to use on the hoodlums who heckled him.

132

THAT WAS SAN FRANCISCO

The second largest gambling casino in the world—the Café Royal, in the basement of what is now the Pacific Building at Fourth and Market; only the casino at Monte Carlo was bigger. Its bouncer was the handsome Paddy Ryan, whom John L. Sullivan defeated for the championship in 1882, and who wore, while on bouncing duty, a silk hat, cutaway coat, flowered vest, and striped pants. But fancy clothes were the rule. Remember when John L. and Jim Corbett fought a four-round exhibition at the Grand Opera House—in swallowtail coats?

And the old Palace Hotel, for decades the most elegant hostelry west of Chicago, full of history and historic incidents. Like the time President Ulysses S. Grant, on his first visit to San Francisco, received such a mighty acclaim as he drove into the rotunda that a Chinese waiter on an upper balcony leaned over to see what all the shouting was about. Only one thing was wrong with this understandable gesture: the waiter forgot he had a tray full of dishes on top of his head. They landed squarely in the President's lap.

And around the Palace they still talk about the day a white man and his Indian wife arrived from Alaska, where he had just dug up a fortune in gold. He wanted nothing but the best, or better, so the manager installed the couple in an elegant suite on the top floor. But lo, the poor Indian wife of the rich miner was so unnerved by the elevator ride that when dinner time came she told her husband to go ahead. She preferred to walk down to the dining room.

A few minutes later she joined her husband at his table,

holding a large hunting knife in her hand. Her explanation was simple: "I blaze trail down to dining room so could find way back after dinner." For six floors she had hacked chunks out of the expensive woodwork and banisters!

Yes, characters, always characters. The tough old-time cops who used to discourage known pickpockets by breaking their hands with one blow from their billies. The Superior Court judges who were known as "Crying Eddie" Shortall (he whined slightly while dressing down attorneys); "Ethical Edgar" Zook (the loophole boys had a tough time with him); and "Rain-in-the-Face" Treadwell, who was part Indian, wore a high collar and shoestring tie, and chewed a mighty wad of tobacco (a man of deadly aim). Scholer Bangs, most renowned of the old lamplighters, who used to fire up the street lamps along Webster Street between California and Sutter, followed by hordes of kimono-clad Japanese kiddies, all chanting: "Limpy, limpy lamplighter, California flea-biter, when the lamps begin to light, then the fleas begin to bite!"

Even at the tender age of six a San Franciscan might well be a character. About to make his first appearance with Alfred Hertz and the San Francisco Symphony, Violinist Yehudi Menuhin decided it was too warm under the spotlights on the Civic Auditorium stage—and made everybody wait while he calmly put down his bow and fiddle, peeled off his white sweater, handed it across the footlights to his father, and then nodded that he was ready to launch his professional career.

134

THAT WAS SAN FRANCISCO

Memories of April 18, 1906, too, the day of the earthquakes and fires and the death of an era. They still talk about John Tait running out of his Powell Street apartment seconds before the building collapsed and dashing like a crazy man to his great café. He stood outside a few seconds and cried with relief because it was still standing. Then he unlocked the front door and walked in—to find that everything but the front wall had been demolished.

They still talk, after all these years, of Tenor Enrico Caruso picking himself up from the floor after the first shock had thrown him out of bed and vowing in a loud and frightened voice: "I will never set foot in San Francisco again!" (Although, obviously, a foot was not what he was setting on San Francisco at the moment.) The little-known sequel to this gaudy fable being that he was all set for a triumphal "home-coming" concert in San Francisco some fifteen years later—only to die an untimely death in Italy.

They like to tell the story of John Barrymore, still clad in white tie and tails, wandering about the shattered city on the morning of April 18 and talking a newspaperman into sending an emergency wire for him to his uncle, John Drew, and his sister, Ethel, in New York. In the telegram John fabricated a doleful tale of jolted out of bed, wandering around the city in a daze, and being forced by a brutal soldier to grab a shovel and work for twelve solid hours. In New York, Ethel read the wire, turned to Uncle John, and smiled: "Do you believe it?" Answered Drew firmly: "Every word. It took an act of God to get him out of bed and the United States Army to put him to work!"

And, if their memories are especially good, they might smile about the opening, just after the fire, of a makeshift opera season at the Chutes Theater at Fulton and Tenth Avenue. It was *Lohengrin*, starring the ultra-buxom Mme. Lucille Nordica. During the performance she fell down a flight of stairs, shaking the stage so palpably that the whole audience rushed frantically into the street, thinking it was another earthquake.

But always, when they talk about the events of April 18, they talk about the courage of the survivors. Few tributes were more to the point than that of Major General A. W. Greeley, the martial law administrator, who wrote: "It is safe to say that 200,000 people were brought to a state of complete destitution. Yet I never saw a woman in tears, nor heard a man whine over his losses."

But it remained for a young man named Larry Harris to capture best the proud, cocky spirit of San Francisco in 1906. He did it with a poem called "The Damndest Finest Ruins," which, I'm sorry to say, few of the city's present generation seem to have heard of. It goes like this:

THE DAMNDEST FINEST RUINS

Put me somewhere west of East Street where there's nothin' left but dust,
Where the lads are all a bustlin' and where everything's gone bust,
Where the buildin's that are standin' sort of blink and blindly stare
At the damndest finest ruins ever gazed on anywhere.

THAT WAS SAN FRANCISCO

Bully ruins—bricks and wall—through the night I've heard you call
Sort of sorry for each other cause you had to burn and fall,
From the ferries to Van Ness you're a God-forsaken mess,
But the damndest finest ruins—nothin' more or nothin' less.

The strangers who come rubberin' and a huntin' souvenirs,
The fools they try to tell us it will take a million years
Before we can get started, so why don't we come to live
And build our homes and factories upon land they've got to give.

"Got to give!" why, on my soul, I would rather bore a hole
And live right in the ashes than even move to Oakland's mole,
If they'd all give me my pick of their buildin's proud and slick
In the damndest finest ruins still I'd rather be a brick!

20.

THE BIG NIGHT

You don't need a calendar or a newspaper to tell you that it's Saturday night.

It's the "different" night of the week in Baghdad-by-the-Bay—the night when the people who stay home most of the time go out on the town, the night when the people who go out every other night lounge in their apartments and riffle through magazines or listen with half an ear to the radio. The veteran rounders are very lofty about Saturday night, of course. They look down on the mobs from their high windows and sneer: "Look at 'em, the suckers. Why, if anybody saw me out on a Saturday night, I'd die, I tellya, die."

But they're the minority, these veterans of the cirrhosian fields, and on Saturday night the majority rules with a ferocious determination to have a good time if it kills them.

Saturday night starts early for those who have only one

night and a few bucks to squander. The hours are precious and the time is short, and as early as 3 P.M. the dead-pan bartenders are mechanically stuffing their glasses with olives and the red-and-orange sign of the old-fashioned. By 5 P.M. the rush is on, and you begin to see the people emerge—the people for whom the Saturday-night binge is as sacred a ritual as the Saturday-night bath once was.

Yes, Saturday night is different. Usually about this time the traffic is slowly creeping out to the Sunset and Richmond —but tonight the Great Messterpiece is reversed and all roads lead to the pubs and the clubs, the dance halls and the theaters.

Everywhere you see the backbone of the community starting to bend—and who cares if they'll soon be broke? This is Saturday night, the Great American Night, the night it's no disgrace to be seen weaving slightly, the night when even the neighborhood's favorite bluenose is supposed to look at you with forgiving eyes and sniff: "Well, I suppose it's all right. Saturday night, you know." So let joy be unconfined; tomorrow we die with a hangover.

Saturday night's citizens are different too. Take the quiet, mild guy behind the shirt counter in a Kearny Street store. He tells you about his little home on Forty-first Avenue (almost paid for) and his wife's fur coat (almost paid for) and his baby (paid for, "I just got the pink slip on her, ho ho"). But on Saturday night he is transformed into a blue zoot-suited carouser, complete with hand-painted tie and five-buck bills and loud demands that you join him for a snort. "C'mon, pal, jus' a short one, pal, 's Saturday night, ain't it?" And his wife, the one you generally see pushing the baby carriage full of groceries. Tonight her blond hair is set in still concrete on top of her pretty head, and a gardenia corsage is tacked onto her fur coat (almost paid for). "Hi, darling," she grins, and you can hear the mascara crackle. "Wha's a good joint to go to from here, huh? Tonight's the night—our kid has a date with a sitter, and is he keeeeyute!"

Yes, they come from all over and they seem to get everywhere, battling the traffic and the mobs with alarming good nature. Six couples in a tiny sedan, whooping gaily through the red light at Powell and Geary. Four kids in a coupé trying to make a U-turn at California and Mason while understanding Copper "Bunny" Higgins watches helplessly and makes clucking noises. Eight young couples from the outer Mission going through the time-honored paces of the pub crawl from door to door along Columbus Avenue. And always, over the whole gorgeous scene, an air of frenzied futility as the clock inches toward 2 A.M.—for as any good Saturday nighter knows, five saloons is par for the course and few break it. Gershwin could have written the unsung, unspoken chant: "One night a week to live, one night a week to live . . ."

Even hard-boiled Skid Road, supposedly immune to anything less than a full-fledged earthquake, gets a touch of Saturday-night fever. The Skid Rowgues find the pickin's easier along Market Street and scuttle back to their favorite Third Street bar to swallow their profits with the spirits in which they were given. A pair of under-age Apple Annies, with a couple of slightly fractured sailors in tow, confide happily to each other: "Chee, kid, sorta reminds ya of th' good ol' nights durin' the war, don't it?" The patrol wagons chalk up hundreds of extra miles, handing out the Haul of Justice, and the veterans of the Shore Patrol begin to talk bitterly of demanding bottle stars for their Mission Street campaign ribbons.

As the hands on the Ferry Building clock stand straight up (a trick beyond the capabilities of most San Francisco at the time) Saturday night hits the peak of its crescendo. The floors in a hundred clubs are littered with cigarette butts and gardenias slowly turning black. The immaculate, dearly bought hair-dos of 7 P.M. have disappeared into swirling creations which even Mme. Medusa might envy, and a dozen guys are examining the spots on their best ties and wondering whether cleaning will save them. On street corners, the couples flip coins to see whether they'll try to catch the midnight movie on Market or wind it all up with waffles and coffee. And in the Mark lobby an old-time habitué looks around at the huge crowd, shrugs, and walks out, flipping to the headwaiter: "Huh—nobody's here."

Saturday night dies slowly, for those who worship it and live for it do their best to keep it alive. But there is a sadness about the revelry now—as though, suddenly, everyone were looking ahead, past the long sleep and the comic sections, to the dreary imminence of Monday and its endless problems.

Slowly the out-of-towners who had their night in "The City" begin the long voyage home, and the bright small talk of a few hours before withers and dies in a gloomy silence. The young couples head for Twin Peaks, Telegraph Hill, and Land's End, to console each other with love and sympathy, and as the first light appears in the east, a young man with coat unbuttoned and tie askew raises his bottle at Powell and California and murmurs: "Good morning, Shunday!"

Already the dark figures are hurrying toward the churches.

21.

HOW TO BE A SAN FRANCISCAN

Nobody likes to feel like an outsider—even in San Francisco, traditionally one of the friendliest of cities.

So, as an invaluable aid to visitors and the city's 200,000 postwar newcomers, I have compiled some of the clichés that will keep even the most casual tourist from saying the wrong thing at the wrong time. If he memorizes the following simple points, he will instantly melt into the scenery as though he'd been there all his life.

For instance:

When you're caught in the middle of a torrential downpour on Market Street (without a raincoat), don't duck into the nearest doorway; stick your chest out, pound it happily, and gurgle to your neighbor: "Ah, this wet fog! There's something so *exhilarating* about it, isn't there?" . . . Never admit in public that you were born in Anamosa, Iowa; when the subject comes up, just look hurt and hedge: "Why, when my father first came to this town, even the ferryboats were horse-drawn" . . . Show that you're in the social swim by announcing loudly and knowingly at dinner parties: "Whew, whatta day! Had lunch with Tookie, played golf this afternoon with Lovey, and had cocktails with Cooey. By the way, anybody seen Budgy lately?"

Never call the bigger hotels by their right names; it's very important to know that you're meeting somebody at the Frantic, or going dancing at the Mark or Drake; when the Fairmont comes up, inquire archly: "You mean Playland-at-the-Beach-on-the-Hill?" . . . Don't let anyone actually catch you enjoying the wonders of Golden Gate Park; if you're cornered near the Aquarium, murmur quickly: "Oh—uh—hello. Just thought I'd cut through the Park. Meeting some dull friends in the Sunset, ha-ha."

Always be prepared when somebody tells you, with the excited air of a twentieth-century Columbus, that the Fife Building is on Drumm street; the stock return is: "Phoo, that's nothing—there's a finance company at One Polk and Two Fell." . . . Beam lovingly every time you see a cable car trundling by, and go on record as preferring exile to the Farallones to life in a cableless San Francisco; but remember never to drive up a hill behind one—unless you have a bunch of tourists with you, in which case you mention casually: "Really scares you when one of these things starts sliding back—wow!" . . . Whenever you pass that parking lot on O'Farrell Street between Powell and Stockton, let a sad look ooze over your face and sigh: "Yep, the old Orpheum. Never forget how my dear old dad used to take me to Saturday matinees. After lunch at Herbert's, of course. Kinda glad they tore the Orpheum down, at that. Be awful if she were still standing—showing second-run movies." If a tear trickles down your cheek at this point, so much the better.

Listen patiently when a visitor remarks, as though he were suddenly struck with a brilliant idea: "Y'know, there are only three cities in the United States"; it is considered quite rude to chorus along with him: "New York, New Orleans, and San Francisco" . . . You are required to reply: "Well, New York is a nice place to visit, but I'd hate to live there. New Orleans? O.K., they got French cooking, and that's all. But San Francisco! This is a nice place for a week end, but I love to live here!" . . . Never let a Professional Old-Timer convince you that the Barbary Coast made Sodom and Gomorrah seem tamer than Minneapolis and St. Paul; just growl back: "Oh yeah? You been boozin' around Lower Mason Street lately?" Chances are he hasn't, so build your own little fable from there.

Never look at Treasure Island without saying dreamily: "Ah, seems like only yesterday that yon drab place was a veritable fairyland of lights, gaiety, laughter, hahahaha. And yet, friend, we have lived a lifetime since then. Now we are old—our dreams as dead as the make-believe palaces that once glittered out there on that man-made magic isle." If you bruise easily, substitute the word: "Gee" . . . Always tell your luncheon dates (if you're a woman) that you'll "meet under the clock at the Frantic" or (if you're a man) "in front of the cigar stand in the Palace." . . . To show that you're *au courant* with the town's greats, always refer to Kathleen Norris as "Aunt Kate." If someone brings up Harry Bridges, you return: "Ah yes, as I was saying to The Nose just the other day . . ." A certain lawyer is just "The Master." When the subject gets around to Wee Willie Saroyan, interrupt dolefully: "I just don't know what's happened to Bill lately. He's a changed man. Never see him around the old spots." Steinbeck you fluff off cruelly with: "Steinbeck. Steinbeck. Oh yes, I remember—wrote a book once, didn't he?"

Always wear a topcoat on a warm day and shiver without one on a cool day, so you can say: "Well, guess I'll never learn. When I left the house this morning it was cool (warm) and now it's warm (cool). But that's the charm of good old San Francisco, I always say, yes, sir." If you always say this often enough, you're likely to wind up as a member of the Bohemian Club . . . Your reaction to Oakland should always be friendly, but tinged with delicate humor, like: "After all, the Bay Bridge had to end *somewhere*." . . . When somebody tells you that it's "impossible" to swim from Alcatraz to the mainland, because of the currents, don't be so rude as to point out that a girl swimmer did it without much trouble a few years back; after all, she hadn't trained on bread and water.

If you go out to Ocean Beach on a Sunday, don't be so naïve as to take along a bathing suit; wear your business suit,

146

roll up your pants, and go wading, with your shoes slung carelessly over your shoulder . . . Even though you are a habitual yawner at 11 P.M., always profess great indignation at our 2 A.M. closing, pointing out wrathfully: "After all, this city has a night-life reputation to keep up—and with all those big conventions coming to town, well, it just doesn't seem right to fold up so early" . . . The first time you hear a tourist say "Frisco," let it float by; if he says it again, lay a firm hand on his arm and advise: "Look, friend, in these here parts we call it San Francisco"; the third time he says the awful word, fix him with a steely glance and rasp: "When you say that, smile, you ———!"

Having complied with all the above rules and regulations, you automatically become a full-fledged San Franciscan and are entitled to begin all conversations with: "Yup, the old town has sure changed. Why, I remember when . . ."

22.

A TALE OF THE TOWN

It was in one of those south o' Market beer joints that always looks like a Saroyan stage set. Reeking delicately of stale beer and half-crowded with the usual assortment of stock characters. You know, the old bag just out of the county jug, trying to act charming for the benefit of a counterfeit Diamond Jim Brady, who has enough scratch to buy her one drink while he is downing three. A couple of slightly younger creations, jabbing at the juke box for a sentimental tune that sounded even shoddier there than it really is. And, of course, the youngish, fairly clean-cut guy sitting on a stool and staring at his glass as though it held the answer to everything.

That was my friend Harry. Well, we'll call him Harry because that happens to be his first name. Last names don't matter anyway. We'd gone into the Army together, become fast friends for a fast week or two, and then he'd gone his way and I'd gone mine.

"Hiya, stranger," I said. "How ya feel?"

"Well, for one thing, I feel like a beer," he answered. "If you're talking about anything else, I feel lower than a snake." I've cleaned that up.

I won't bore you with the next few minutes. We went through the ordinary line of talk, bringing each other up to date. No doubt of it, he'd been through plenty. "Seems they couldn't make an invasion without me," was the GI way he put it. Casablanca, Sicily, and then to the Pacific for Eniwetok, Saipan, and finally Leyte.

"You must have more fruit salad than Eisenhower," I suggested.

He fished in his pocket and arranged a couple of rows of ribbons on the bar, lining them up with elaborate neatness. Among other things, the Silver Star and its automatic companion, the Purple Heart.

He took another drink of beer, all the while contemplating the ribbons. "Nice going," I said. He nodded. "You know how we used to kid about these things," he said.

"Sure. With those, and a nickel, you could get a cup of coffee. Only now it takes a dime."

"Well, I never quite believed that," he said slowly, evening up the ribbons to a mathematical nicety. "But the other day a buddy and I got tanked up and decided to find out. We went into four beaneries on Market and laid our ribbons down and told 'em we wanted something to eat—and they could keep the ribbons for security. They looked at us like we were crazy or somethin'. Maybe we were. Are."

I'm afraid I didn't have anything to say. But he did.

"But hell, that's not what I'm feelin' brought down about. A couple of hours ago I had three cents in my pocket. Literally. Now I've got a few bucks. The way I got it, that's what brings me down."

"Steal it?" I asked.

"Think I'd feel bad about that?" he answered. "No. I ran into another buddy of mine. He told me how we both could make four bucks. Y'know how? Very simple, he says. You just go to that blood place around the corner, they prick your finger for a blood test and take your pressure, and if you're okay they take a pint of blood and when you walk out, they hand you four George Washingtons."

He stopped and rubbed a finger over the Purple Heart.

"Well, I didn't wanta do it, but what the hell. I lost more than a pint fightin' the war, anyway. And this purple thing won't getcha a flop and a square like four bucks will. So I said okay.

"We went up to the joint at the corner, by the blood place, and he bought me a beer. He said you can pay me back when you get the four bucks—you look healthy. Ever feel like a prize steer? That's the way I felt."

I thought that was the end of the story, but no.

"Say, you remember Captain Hurley, don'tcha?" he asked in what seemed like a change of mood and subject.

"Sure," I said. "Fat character. Found a home in the Army."

"Well, he was in that saloon at the corner. In civvies. The joker gave me the brush off. I know he saw me, but he turned his back. At first I thought he was playing big shot. But I guess he was just embarrassed. 'Cause when me and my buddy got in line for the blood test, behind about fifty winos and stuff, who's up there ahead of us? Buckin' the line as usual. Captain Hurley. Still makin' the enlisted men wait."

He laughed at his own joke.

"That's about all there is to it. You go inside and sign some forms and then you go into a room where a bunch of guys are laid out like stiffs. There's nothing much to it—no pain or anything. And after a few minutes you get up and they ask if you want coffee, and then you get the four bucks."

"Doesn't sound too bad," I offered, looking at my beer glass and turning it around and around.

"I'd rather starve to death than do it again," he said. "Oh —funny thing struck me while I was standing in line. Right across the street from this blood place there's a newspaper office. I kept wondering if they knew that the best human-interest story in town was going on—right in their laps."

I grinned and shrugged. "By the way," I said, "didja see any more of Captain Hurley?"

Harry picked up his ribbons and put them back in his pocket.

"I saw him on the way out. Know what? He couldn't pass the blood test—howdya like that? I saw him after, standing on the corner, shaking his head sort of. So I slipped him a buck. And by God he took it."

Well, that's about all there is to the story. Out on the sidewalk, with the juke box still dinning away in the background, we shook hands and said good-by. I watched him walk away, with his left hand in his pocket—the one with the ribbons in it.

23.

THE CITY: ONCE OVER LIGHTLY

THE SIGHTS: A metropolis in motion on a wet and foggy night—the cars sliding backward down the slick bricks of Powell, looking frantic and helpless; the gripmen halting their cable cars to wipe off the front windows, a gesture as futile as trying to empty the Bay with a jigger; girl'n'boysterous kids on the North Beach slopes of Russian Hill, going through the elaborate motions of skiers as they skid giddily down the steep slidewalks; and goose-pimply pedestrians, turning up their coat collars and plunging their hands into their pockets in what seems to be one continuous gesture.

The vacant lots behind the smart apartment houses of Nob Hill, filled with dirt and dust and papers and scurrying rats—a breeding place for disease in the district of good breeding . . . The sagging wooden houses along Eddy and Ellis in the Western Addition—quaint and picturesque only to those who don't have to half-live a life inside their musty, dusty hulks . . . And the tiny side-street hotels on the tattered fringes of the business district—boasting that they're "just around the corner from everything," and filled with lonely people who've long since given up trying to get around that corner, to anything.

THE SOUNDS: The 5 A.M. clang and clatter of the scavengers—rushing to clean up their dirty work before the alarm-clocktail hour . . . The friendly chuckle of the loose bricks under the wheels of your car on California Street—old and battered cobbles bearing up bravely under a great load . . . The strident community singing in the Gay Nineties, flooding the International Settlement every time the front door swings open, then stopping with knife-like suddenness when the door closes . . . The agonized groans of the Ferry Building's wooden pilings as a ferry shoulders its way in, each splinter crying as though its back were about to break . . . The roar of the gore at Kearny and Market, where traffic leaps at each other from all sides and your subconscious, in sudden retreat, drops a curtain over your ears to shut out the honking of geese who drive cars . . . The Chinese children playing shrilly-nilly in their picturesque playground along Sacramento Street, each one screaming as though to prove that his lungs have already grown up . . . Grace Cathedral's muscular carillon loading the air with grace notes that hang heavy for long minutes before they die out to allow another to cry out . . . The downtown doormen at the rush hour, standing at street corners and blowing their tin whistles for cabs that have already been caught with their flags down.

THE SMELLS: The smoky-dokey nosegay of spareribs that saturates the night air along Post near Fillmore, so heavy that you can almost sniff a full order of odor . . . That definable "public building" snootful that smacks you square in the smeller whenever you enter the old Post Office at Seventh and Mission—a conglomeration of age, heat, bodies, and disinfectant adding up to something your nose would rather not hear about . . . The not-so-mysterious new car smell around most of the "used" cars on the Van Ness lots—a perfume you can own for lots and lots . . . That fried-in-deep-fatmosphere that comes pouring out of too many downtown restaurants—providing a preview of indigestion . . . The clean, woody breath of Mount Davidson where you can fill your lungs with high octane and wish that you had room for more . . . The deep, cloying whiff of the ages that lurks in the back alleys of the Portsmouth Square sector—a something-in-the-air that seems almost as palpable as the ancient buildings that exude it; nosetalgic, you might call it . . . Skid Road's stale beer, Broadway's chile and hamburgers, the Beach's popcorn salted with sea spray, the real perfume that comes to your senses in Grant Avenue's chicspots, Fisherman's Wharf's shrimp à la noseburg, the air alive with jave jive in the "Coffee Belt" under the Bay Bridge—these are the signposts you can see with your eyes closed in Baghdad-by-the-Bay.

THE CHARACTERS: The "cat man" who drops into Joe Ruben's barbershop on O'Farrell just to spin fabulous fables of felines for the amusement of the customers—who laugh as loudly as they dare, considering the razors at their throats . . . Tessie, the tired and retired flame of the Tenderloin, still trying to flicker up some interest in the all-night saloons —and more hateful than grateful if you'll merely condescend to buy her a drink; her fountain of youth is dry, but the bourbon helps a little . . . The faceless old men who sit shoulder to shoulder, yet worlds apart, on the benches of Union Square, their downcast eyes fastened on a passing parade of ankles; overhead, the Dewey Monument—like a gravestone in this cemetery of the living dead . . . The blind, banjo-playing beggar of Market Street, who strums as hard on your heartstrings as he does on his instrument; the songs he shouts are almost as old as the Muniserable streetcars that rattle by—and drown him out . . . The Marina housewives who shop in their slacks, the merchants who moan that it's slack in their shops, the Montgomery Street stenos who worry about their diets on starvation wages, their thin bosses dining on thick steaks at the Blue Fox, the rat-faced black marketeers who can't get adjusted to "civilian" life, the grinning political candidates who try to remember your name so you'll remember theirs at the polls.

These are some of the citizens of Baghdad-by-the-Bay, where it takes all kinds to make this world we call a city.

24.

COCKTAILS FOR TWO THOUSAND

Time was when the merest whisper of the word "Los Angeles" in San Francisco would provoke a riot. But that was long, long ago, when all California seemed to be in imminent danger of being overrun by the city with the nervous boundaries.

Now that Los Angeles has come to mean "Hollywood," all that has changed. Throwing self-respect to the winds, San Franciscans admit openly to having spent a week end in the Colossus of Southern California, returning home to regale the natives with wild tales of seeing Lana Turner in a dress "way down to here," and movie heroes sprawled in dark night-club corners with marijuana cigarettes drooping carelessly from their lips.

After its own fashion Hollywood observes this new rapport between the cities by "world-premièring" some of its worst pictures in San Francisco, complete with personal appearances by the featured performers. I wish I could say that sophisticated, cosmopolitan San Francisco rises above these obvious blandishments, *mais non*. But no. The newest generation of dwellers by the Bay, throwing self-respect to the winds, gape and gawk and succumb like the scroungiest Los Angeleno.

Inevitably these periodic rites call for that lovable Twentieth-century institution, the cocktail party, where the producers and their stars open the gates of their hearts to the press and public and declare that they're "so happy to be in San Francisco" and that "San Francisco is my favorite city." Don't you believe it.

For a typical picture of Hollywood-in-action-in-San-Francisco you might have stepped recently into the Green Room of Hotel St. Francis, where you would have found an incredibly thirsty mob drinking its way through a forest of highball glasses and cutting through acres of hors d'oeuvres, all thoughtfully provided by Mr. Darryl Zanuck.

Mr. Zanuck himself couldn't be there, but he paid the check, and out of his great-heartedness was supposed to come oodles of good will for a new (and now forgotten) motion picture called *My Darling Clementine*, whoever she is. Or was.

While cocktail parties are not exactly my favorite indoor sport, Mr. Zanuck's production was an outstanding example of this peculiar social phenomenon. Besides being jammed to the door with people nobody ever heard of, it boasted such vibrant personalities as Georgie Jessel, Cathy Downs, Nancy

Guild, Lon McAllister, Peggy Ann Garner, Vivian Blaine, and Kurt Kreuger, all of whom have something to do with the movies, plus a few wandering musicians who strolled around playing "My Darling Clementine," from the picture of the same name.

As soon as I approached the Green Room (so-called because of its gold walls), I sensed that this was no ordinary Martini-bake. Clustered outside the door were a dozen or so infants, all clutching autograph books, dry pens, and broken pencils, and frantically scrutinizing each oncoming face. These, I was interested to note, were the same children who hang around every local gathering of celebrities, so I asked the spokesman, Jay Thompson, a chubby young man of serious mien, how his group happens to find out about these events.

"Well," he explained kindly, "we all belong to the Fan Clubs of America, Incorporated, and we have a secret system for locating movie stars. As soon as one of us finds out there are stars in town, the word is flashed to all the members and we send out a task force to cover it. Incidentally, we're having our national convention here next month, and we do hope you'll attend. Now sign my book and you may go."

I signed my name and was released, while his comrades clustered around him, looked at my signature, and asked one another with various indications of perplexity: "Who's that?"

Inside, the scene already was one of wildest confusion. One was immediately reminded of old paintings of Rome at the height of the orgy season. Rome, New York, that is. There were so many press agents from Twentieth Century-Fox that

159

in the turmoil they lost their identities and began telling one another about the virtues of *My Darling Clementine*. Listening to their conversations, you'd have thought that Darryl Zanuck invented the Twentieth Century, when everybody knows it was the New York Central.

I don't know where all the people came from, but I know what they were looking for. Movie stars, that's what. Every two seconds some character dribbling caviar and bourbon down his shirt front would walk up to me, look me up and down, and then walk away, grunting nastily: "Nyaaah, another nobody."

After being labeled a nobody for the fifth time, a terrible feeling of shame and guilt swept over me, and I walked around apologizing to the various scrutinizers, who turned out to be fairly sympathetic and only beat me where it doesn't show.

Finally, after twelve cases of scotch, twenty cases of bourbon, and enough Martinis to float 3000 olives had been consumed, the somebodies burst dramatically onto the scene. The guests immediately clustered around them, uttering little, glad cries.

Mr. Jessel, dressed all in gray to match the flecks at his temples, flitted around like a veteran, shaking hands two at a time and keeping up an impressive running commentary. "Ah, the St. Francis," he said. "Haven't been here for thirty years and it hasn't changed a bit. Not an improvement in sight."

"Say, little Peggy Ann Garner," he said to little Peggy Ann Garner, "have you ever been in San Francisco before?"

160

Her lips formed the single syllable "No." "Well," went on the irrepressible George, "I'm gonna take you down and show you around the old Barbary Coast. Then when you're four years older, I'll tell you what used to go on down there!"

Miss Nancy Guild (rhymes with wild) confided that she was just wuild (rhymes with Guild) about San Francisco, and Miss Cathy Downs, who plays "Clementine," said she thought our town's (rhymes with Downs) the tops. Kurt Kreuger and Lon McAllister made it unanimous.

The party might have lasted all night except that even Darryl Zanuck can't keep 1100 people supplied with scotch indefinitely. As the glasses emptied, interest in *My Darling Clementine* drooped from fever pitch to just mild frenzy, and the guests began stealing away, some of them clutching pieces of paper on which were written such memorabilia as "Bestest, Peggy Ann Garner," and "Sincerely, Lon McAllister." One prominent San Franciscan was gingerly holding a whole envelope full of these signatures, and reporting proudly: "Gee, wait till my kid sees this. Will she be jealous!"

I might say that I turned slightly green myself, and for a split, insane second considered hitting him on the head, snatching the precious envelope, and running like sixty.

Instead, I just ran like sixty out the door, through the lobby, and skidded to a halt on Powell Street, where I sniffed the cool night air and noted with relief that the cable cars were still running and that the sidewalks were filled with nobodies.

I hope the doorman isn't still wondering why I asked him for his autograph.

25.

THESE ARE SAN FRANCISCANS

In my column I do a lot of talking about "typical San Franciscans."

You may smile, if you like, and tell me there's no such animal—but I'll argue with you. We may differ about their characteristics, but if they live long enough in any of the various districts of the city, they soon take on certain mannerisms, a rather special outlook, and at least a few recognizable attributes.

By "typical," I don't necessarily mean the artist who might live on Telegraph Hill, or the Homburg-hatted clubman stepping into his brownstone retreat on Nob Hill. Although these types have come to be associated with those locations, they're almost caricatures today. I have in mind a more average San Francitizen.

Maybe I can describe him best this way:

THESE ARE SAN FRANCISCANS

If he thinks that his section of town is the true heart of San Francisco and that his neighbors are the only real people for miles around . . . And if he talks with an accent that is slightly on the cocky side and yet not unpleasant . . . And if he proudly demonstrates that he can walk down the main drag of his district and call at least every other passerby by his first name—he's a young man of the Mission.

(But on Saturday night he's quite likely to be found drinking in the Mark bar and hoping that nobody will notice that he's from what he hears is the "wrong" side of the streetcar tracks.)

If he gets highly annoyed when he hears people say that Telegraph Hill affords the best view in town . . . And if he immediately stutters to the defense by pointing out that his location is much more accessible and that the rents are more sensible and that his neighborhood is more genuinely colorful . . . And if he tries to clinch his anti-Telegraph Hill argument by pointing out that a cable line traverses *his* mountain—he gets his thrills and bills on Russian Hill.

(But when he has visitors up to his apartment, he never fails to lure them out onto his back balcony by calling: "Take a look—isn't this a wonderful view of Coit Tower?")

If he can rattle off a dozen reasons why it's a great advantage to live on the flat of the land in this hilliest of metropolises . . . And if he likes the way the streets are staggered so there are few dangerous intersections for his children to cross . . . And if, on pleasant evenings, he usually strolls past the gently rocking boats in Yacht Harbor and says to

163

his wife: "Now where else in San Francisco can you take a nice walk without having to climb a hill?"—he lives his life in the Marvelous Marina.

(But near the end of one of those walks with his wife he catches himself looking up at the imposing homes stacked on the bluff of Pacific Heights and murmuring: "Someday, darling, we'll live in one of those big houses—on that hill.")

If he wears the kind of clothes you call "sharp" and sprinkles his conversation with such "fly" talk as "Man, you look ready tonight. Me, I'm feelin' George, strictly George" . . . And if he regards the customs and habits of the older folks in his neighborhood with something less than tolerance at times, and insists that the only thing to do is to get hep and be American and forget about that ancient stuff . . . And if he feels pretty good about the fact that he can call a lot of prominent whites by their first names and get a like greeting in return—he's one of the young Americhinese of Chinatown.

(But now and then he sits alone over a drink at Li-Po and wonders why the landlord took just one look at his face and slammed the door when he tried to rent an apartment a few blocks outside his district.)

If he's a bull-lunged booster for one of the newest and most virile cities within this city . . . And if he likes his particular view of the Bay because it's "different" and you get a "unique slant on the Bridge" . . . And if he's quick to point out that the bars and restaurants are often patronized by "people from downtown," and that the whites and Negroes and Chinese get along fine as neighbors, and that right over there is one of the town's biggest industries with thousands of workers on a monthly pay roll in the millions—he lives, laughs, and loves in the Bay View district at Hunters Point.

(But he's not quite sure whether the most important point of all the points he points out is named after a couple of Hunters or a couple of hunters.)

If the quickest way to make him blow his topper is to remind him that his district might be designated as a "slum area" and be razed for modern housing units . . . And if he always insists that he's happy the 1906 fire didn't leap across Van Ness Avenue to wipe out some of the most historic homes in town ("and isn't it awful that some of them are just boardinghouses now?") . . . And if he likes to relate the colorful background of the particular house he lives in, and describes its parquet floors and its filigree gewgaws and its quaint cupola and the long, winding staircase—he's an Eastern addition to the Western Addition.

(But he invariably neglects to mention that thirty-two people live in that great old house with him.)

If there's a tinge of self-consciousness in the way he resents big-city wisecracks about his little community . . . And if he angrily snaps that he pays only a $1.29 tax rate, and merely a dollar a month for his water, and just ten cents a month for garbage removal . . . And if he wants you to notice the big front and back yard surrounding his house, and the nearby shopping center and theater—he's a borderline San Franciscan who lives in Daly City.

(But when he *really* wants to impress a city slicker with the charm of his burg, he adds: "And besides, we have just as many bookie joints as you. Per capita, that is!")

If you can detect a superior curl to his lip as he casually drops the name of the fortunate section of town he inhabits . . . And if you can recognize from his chit-chatter that he rubs a neighborly and very square shoulder with some of our best-known moneybags . . . And if he's not bashful about giving the impression that he's a logical successor to the area once tenanted by the Hopkinses and the Stanfords and the Floods and the Crockers—he's a princely being who heads each night for his magic minaret atop fabled Nob Hill.

(But don't expect him to invite you along for a drink, for then you'd discover he lives in a two-room furnished apartment, right around all the wrong corners of the hill that holds its nose in the air.)

If his favorite way of irritating his fellow workers at the office is to offer: "Yeah? Well, I'll betcha I get to *my* place before you get out to the Sunset, and here's a green picture of Abe Lincoln that says so" . . . And if he just can't get over the fact that he paid less than nothing for his lot and house and has plenty of privacy . . . And if he'll be darned if he can understand why thousands of San Franciscans don't flock over to his bailiwick when it's really nothing but a five-minute spin across the Bridge—he's the guy who acts like he discovered Marin County.

(But after he's had dinner, plus one too many, at your house in the Sunset, he never fails to yawn: "Ya don't mind

166

if I just curl up on yer sofa and sleep here, do ya? Honist, I'm not up to that long drive across the Bridge tonight!")

These are "typical" San Franciscans. I know because I've met every one of them—a thousand times in a hundred places.

26.

DOWN WHERE THE TALL GARLIC GROWS

The center of North Beach, which isn't a beach, is Washington Square, which isn't a square and which doesn't contain a statue of Washington but of Benjamin Franklin. That observation is Newsman Kevin Wallace's, and it's as good a way as any to get into the merry hodgepodge that is San Francisco's Italian-Bohemian sector.

"Little Italy" is the most colorful foreign colony in the city, Chinatown not excepted. Its Italian flavor is as real as the garlic that hangs in clouds along the streets where the hamburgers are thick on slices of French bread and the waiters drown their salads in wine vinegar and the pots of spaghetti are filled and refilled a dozen times a day.

Chinatown puts on a garish oriental front to impress tourists. North Beach makes no particular attempt to Americanize itself, nor do its residents go out of their way to please the visitor—and so, perversely, it pleases everybody, including the native San Franciscans.

It is a section as genuinely Italian as the firm name of Lavezzo Bros., Bacigalupi & Brachetto, mfrs. of ravioli, taglierini, and tortellino. It is a section of old, large, and fiercely loyal families who speak only Italian at the dinner table, who intermarry, who amass fortunes but go on living in the house their father built forty years ago. It is an earthy, somewhat rough section where the bootleggers once flourished and the Mafia still strikes occasional terror, and both the funerals and the weddings are big and costly.

But North Beach is more than the district where thousands of Italians live much as their fathers lived in the old country. Its restaurants draw thousands into the section nightly. So do its bars, featuring *caffe espresso* and *cappuccino*, hot drinks made in huge, shiny, steaming things apparently designed by an Italian Rube Goldberg. In a saloon called the Bocce Ball hopeful young North Beach sopranos and tenors sing operatic arias to the accompaniment of an accordion, and occasionally go on to jobs in the opera chorus. At Finocchio's the tourists gawk at male performers dressed like women, and at Mona's they gape at women who are dressed like men. In Original Andy's barbershop the men go to have their hair cut long and a finger wave set in, and at the Black Cat, 12 Adler Place, and the Iron Pot the artists whose hair grows long anyway dream their dreams over drinks provided by the most practical kind of art patrons.

The restaurants are big, bright, and colorful, their tables

heaped with the inevitable, indigestible Italian hors d'oeuvres and stacks of thick-sliced French bread. Chances are you'll find yourself drinking red wine whether you like it and order it or not. You'll go out feeling overstuffed, but the check will be surprisingly low, in most cases, and you'll probably have met the owner, who will turn out to be a character combining all the best qualities of Sam Goldwyn and the late Henry Armetta.

One thing about the Italian restaurateurs—they aren't dull. At Lupo's, where the pizza makes your heart sing and burn in equal proportions, Frankie Cantalupo thinks nothing of getting down on his knees to convince you to try a side order of pickled squid. At John's Rendezvous you're likely to find John Sobrato addressing Bing Crosby as "Bink" and getting highly insulted when "Bink" refused to step out on the floor and sing a few numbers for the folks. And at Vanessi's the ineffable Joe Vanessi himself will seat himself casually at your table and be calling you by your first name before the meal is half over.

Vanessi is a man who is beautifully unimpressed by celebrities. One night Marlene Dietrich walked in alone, took a seat at the counter, and ordered a hamburger. Over to her walked Vanessi, who said dourly enough: "You Miss Dietrich, no? A few months back my wife makes me take her to the Cocoanut Grove, on account she hears you gonna be there and she just wants to see you walk in. So you come in for a few minutes and walk out. It costs me $22. Now you come to San Francisco, you order a hamburger, and you get to see *me*—for thirty-five cents!"

DOWN WHERE THE TALL GARLIC GROWS

Who but Joe Vanessi would think of calling John Charles Thomas "Charlie," which he did one recent evening to Thomas's delight and fascination. Who but Vanessi would be so charmingly confused as to call up the newspapers to report that "the great Willie Hoppe himself, in person, was just in and now he's across the street in that little Filipino pool hall, shootin' pool. Yeah, Willie Hoppe!" Newspapermen who dropped around to watch Billiard Champion Hoppe playing in a tiny North Beach poolroom discovered it wasn't Hoppe at all. Merely some radio comedian named Bob Hope.

While he was playing an engagement in a San Francisco hotel, Bandleader Artie Shaw suffered so horribly from insomnia that he used to keep Joe up all night every night, just to have somebody to talk to. One sleepless night, after Shaw had kept Joe up till 7 A.M., Vanessi complained: "I no canna unnerstan' you, Ottie. You're top man in your business, you gotta lotta money, you're smart, you're handsome, and the girls are nuts about you. Why—if I was you, I'd sleep all day!"

The only celebrity who made life miserable for Vanessi was the famed writer of sea stories, the late Albert Richard Wetjen, who strolled into the restaurant one night, downed a sumptuous meal, and then wound up with a request for crêpes suzette. So Joe set a tray alongside Wetjen's table and went to work on the delicate pancakes, finally winding up by dousing the works with the customary brandy. Then, for the fillip, he set fire to the concoction—at which point Wetjen ordered Vanessi away and sat there elaborately warming his hands in front of the leaping blue flames until they died away and the dessert burned down to a dismal crisp.

Wetjen arose, paid the check, and left, explaining to the sizzling Vanessi: "I just *love* an open fire!"

The name Joe, incidentally, is a moniker of some importance in North Beach, owing not entirely to the eminence of Joltin' Joe DiMaggio. One of the more popular restaurants is called "New Joe," which became so widely known that it soon inspired an imitator who called himself "Original Joe," and that, in turn, spawned a branch known as "Original Joe No. 2," a neat trick and they did it. Thus we find that "Original Joe" is newer than, and not as original as, "New Joe." The confusion became complete recently when what should open across the street from "New Joe's" but a restaurant that calls itself "Original Junior."

However, now that you're all straightened out again, it should be recorded that there's nobody named Joe at "New Joe's." The whole Joe business started many years ago when a Joe Merello opened a cardroom on Broadway in the heart of North Beach. In order to have a "screen" that might confuse the police, he installed a tiny hamburger shop in the front of the place. Just a few stools and one cook—but what hamburgers! Nested in hollowed-out slices of toasted French bread, crisply coated with fried onions, oozing with gobs of butter.

Word of these superburgers spread over San Francisco by word-of-mouthful. Soon customers were stacked three deep behind each stool, their hungry eyes peering over each muncher's shoulder. The delighted cook, Pete Arrigoni, promptly bought out Merello and his cardroom and expanded. He named his place "New Joe," indicating that old Joe Merello was no longer around.

Another classic North Beach delicacy was invented at New Joe's—an unlikely mishmosh called a "Joe's Special." Its birth was pure accident and invention, fathered by a rising young bandleader named Bunny Burson, who was tragically killed at a Peninsula party shortly after. Bunny walked into Joe's for a hamburger one night, only to be told that not enough hamburger was left for a sandwich.

"So whatcha got back there?" asked Burson.

"Oh," shrugged the cook, looking around, "just a coupla eggs, a little hamburger—and—and—some spinach."

"Fair enough," said Burson. "Mix 'em together and fry it in a little oil."

That was the first "Joe's Special." Now it's featured on the menus of a dozen Italian restaurants by that same name.

Another famous North Beach Joe was the proprietor, for a good many years, of a little hideaway called Joe's Wine Cellar, at the foot of Green Street on Telegraph Hill. At this Joe's it was sometimes possible to get a drink after the legal 2 A.M. closing hour. But every now and then the police would put the "heat" on law evaders, and Joe would have to close, like everybody else.

On such unhappy occasions latecomers would find a sad, simple sign hanging on Joe's padlocked front door. Just two words. "Joe sick."

Such is life in North Beach, where There's No Business Like Joe Business.

What's left of San Francisco's Bohemia is centered in North Beach. Once there was Poppa Coppa, who satisfied the palates of half the starving artists in town. Once there were rows of studios on Telegraph Hill, but now they're gone, too, and in their places stand $200-a-month "studio" apartments. And once there was Izzy Gomez.

Izzy was a big, fat Portuguese gentleman of indeterminate age and indescribable largeness of heart. He had two weaknesses. One was for a dirty black wide-brimmed hat which he wore at all times—even, reputedly, in his bath. His other weakness was for people of talent, real or fanciful, who needed a drink or a meal. They could get both in Izzy Gomez's upstairs joint on Pacific Street, and not even a "thank you" was expected.

It was inevitable that a man such as Izzy Gomez should be long on friends and short on money. In fact, somebody else's hat (not his; he wouldn't take it off that long) had to be passed every year to raise the money for his liquor license. To me, it always seemed a little strange that such a banal scrap of commercial paper as a license was even needed at Izzy Gomez's. It wasn't that kind of place. The din of a hundred people drinking and eating was seldom broken by the hard clang of the cash register. Sometimes he seemed positively embarrassed at the act of picking your money up off the bar. "Aw, go on," he would mumble, shoving it back at you. "You my friend!"

DOWN WHERE THE TALL GARLIC GROWS

In a town that loves characters, Izzy was a celebrity. Such esteemed chroniclers of notables as O. O. McIntyre, Walter Winchell, and Lucius Beebe were among his short-order biographers. His down-at-the-heels saloon, which was infinitely more colorful than sanitary, attracted more than the artists he carried on the cuff. Tourists came by the dozens every night. Socialites in mink dotted the bar. Anita Howard Vanderbilt arrived one time wearing, among other jewelry, a bracelet containing a topaz the size of an egg. "Say, lady," said a hanger-on at the next stool, peering curiously at her wrist, "shouldn't you have that thing lanced?" Anita stomped out in a highly perfumed dudgeon with an automatic top.

One of the charming things about the late Izzy was that he never quite saw his saloon as others saw it. It was, to say the least, untidy. It boasted a never-changing rich, ripe fragrance that bore no resemblance to expensive colognes. Dr. J. C. Geiger, the city health director, was occasionally seen staring thoughtfully at the glasses behind the bar.

But to Izzy his place was the last word in swank. It was only after tourists began to flock into his joint, murmuring "how quaint, how colorful," that he began to worry about its appearance. It was a memorable night. Izzy stood in front of the bar, deep reflection apparent in his bright eyes. Then he turned to Newspaperman Neil Hitt and wondered: "Neil, do you suppose if I sprinkled some sawdust around I could make this place look like a dive?"

Since the end of the war that changed the world, even the world of San Francisco, "bohemianism" of the kind typified by the Izzy Gomezes and the Poppa Coppas has died out, along with (figuratively, I hope) the traditional starving artist.

The "arty" hangouts of today are not quite so colorful, perhaps, but a good deal more realistic. Thanks mainly to the efforts of an earnest little Frenchman named Henri Lenoir, such artists' saloons as No. 12 Adler Place, which he operates, and the Iron Pot and the Black Cat act as cut-rate museums for paintings executed by their patrons. Credit for drinks is still extended, but not quite so far. And all three places do exceedingly well on the patronage of "outsiders," who come in nowadays to look at the products of the starving artist as well as the starving artist himself.

On the menus of the Iron Pot you'll find this lovely "Notice to tourists: For Bohemian atmosphere, go to Bohemia. The male customers who need a haircut are not artists. The paintings and prints displayed here are for sale. Limit: one dozen to a customer. But don't ask the help to explain them to you. They don't understand them, either."

Getting back to the aforementioned Lenoir, his stature as a leader of San Francisco's Bohemia dates back only a couple of years, to the time he took over No. 12 Adler Place. As recently as 1946 he was as lean and hungry as any of his confreres, as witness this memo which I published last year, exactly as it was sent to me, and which he subsequently confirmed:

Henri Lenoir was at an afternoon reception given by Mr. Crocker. Among other things there were piles of sandwiches. Henri, starving

176

as usual, began to wolf these down by the handful, and, mindful of lean hours ahead, shoved a few into his pocket. Challenged by a stranger standing by the table, Lenoir merely stared coldly at him and stalked away. The stranger turned out to be his host, Mr. Crocker. Dizzy with embarrassment, Lenoir was tiptoeing out when he was stopped by a gentleman with a ruddy face and a brown suit, who genially asked the fugitive for a match. Henri hastily plunged his hand into his pocket and proffered a sandwich to—Mayor Lapham. Henri fled.

Next to Lenoir's spot on Adler Place, incidentally, is an upstairs "studio" apartment, at No. 10, which for a couple of years bore this sign on its front door: "Please do not ring bell before 3:30 P.M. unless you are a beautiful woman or want to buy a painting." The occupants: Spike Dunavon, a writer (interested in beautiful women), and Mel Fowler, an artist (interested in selling a painting). About a year ago Fowler got married to a beautiful woman who rang the bell in search of a painting. Defeated but gallant, Dunavon presented the couple with the ultimate in wedding gifts—his half of the apartment.

Neo-Bohemia's third concentrating camp for intellectuals is a smoky cavern called the Black Cat, which has some of the thick and suspicious atmosphere that used to distinguish Izzy's trap. The Black Cat is usually being picketed, because the bartenders act as waiters, or vice versa, and there's a rickety piano which no professional is hired to play (there are plenty of volunteer amateurs, however), and also a cigarette machine that continues to vend packages for fifteen cents despite the fact that the tariff is twenty cents everywhere else.

177

The omnipresent pickets at the Cat have no complaints, however. Proprietor Sol Stoumen has kindly provided a carpet for them to walk on in front of his door, and he hands them drinks every night, plus an annual turkey dinner on the house.

The Black Cat, like its counterparts, is regularly invaded by hoity-toity slumming parties, most of whom have various loud and disparaging remarks to make before they sweep out of the place and back into the fresh air. It was a female member of the lifted-pinky set who one night ordered a scotch and soda, examined the glass closely and sourly, and then demanded of Mac, the bartender: "I say, young man, these glasses are sterilized, are they not?"

"Of course, madame," replied Mac graciously. "You're a stranger here, but we always try to protect our regular customers."

There is one little corner of North Beach that has always confused me. At Pacific and Mason, right on the fringe of the Italian colony, are grouped the Pacific Sukiyaki Japanese restaurant, the Normandie French restaurant, the Xochimilco Mexican restaurant, and Jade Snow Wong's Chinese pottery shop. No Italian place of any kind. There is, however, in the midst of all this, an establishment that wisely calls itself "The Neutral Cleaners."

27.

SUNDAY IN THE PARK

Golden Gate Park—a lush anomaly in an overcrowded metropolis. Over a thousand man-made acres, sprawled in a long rectangle between the Sunset and Richmond districts. More than a park—a tradition. Where your mother and father held hands and walked along the shaded, winding paths that look as though they've been there for centuries. Where the dashing ghosts of an earlier generation gallop along the bridle paths, and there are memories in every leafy corner.

Golden Gate Park on a sunny Sunday afternoon. Still the place to go (when in doubt) for thousands of San Franciscans. Still the place where you can lose yourself a thousand miles from the city in a matter of minutes. That wonderful feeling of being "away from everything" as soon as you hit Fell and Baker streets, swing into the Panhandle, and watch the city's grayness fade away and the Park's glorious green-ness slowly grow around you—until even the rattle of the streetcars is lost in the hush of towering trees.

Every Sunday, every year—the same sights, the same sounds.

The jam-packed cars ripping along the Main Drive almost bumper to bumper—each one containing a wife in the back seat who rasps, at various annoying intervals, "Now, Hennery, stop gawking at the scenery and keep your eyes on the car in front of you."

The tourists who crane their necks this way, then that, and finally ruin the afternoon by complaining: "I'm disappointed. They call this Golden Gate Park and yuh can't even see the Gate. I wish we'd gone to a movie instead."

The almost too nostalgic "Portals of the Past" on the shores of sleepy Lloyd Lake—and the venerable Sunday sunners who can tell you, without even consulting their notes, "That's right, m'boy, those marble pillars once were the façade of the Towne mansion at Taylor and California. Yep, they were left standing after the great earthquake and fire back in '06. Those were some days, m'boy, let me tell you."

The night-club characters (you can tell them by their white faces and broad-shouldered suits) who head for the Park every sunny Sunday, grab a bench, and sit for hours with their faces turned skyward—hoping, yearning, dreaming that they're magically becoming sun-tanned Adonises. The almost-sacred Arboretum, forbidden to cars, dogs, and bicycles—an out-of-this-world corner of the Other World that is Golden

SUNDAY IN THE PARK

Gate Park, a hushed paradise of trees and shrubs in an open-air hothouse (when a good dog dies, does he go to an Arboretum?). And the perennial pudgy blond (in slacks, of course) who watches the kiddies riding the donkeys and then says to her boy friend in a petulant whine: "Gee, I wisht I could have a ride on them animules!"

The very ordinary cows "on display" in the children's playground—for the benefit of city kiddies who crowd around and agree learnedly among themselves that "Yessirree, they look just like the cows in the pictures." The large signs near the bridle paths: "Stop, When Horses Cross"—and the omnipresent wag who never fails to chortle: "Yeah, but how do you tell when they're cross?"

The deer in the mid-Park enclosure, who are fed so much guck and junk each Sunday that a certain Sunset District character stops each Monday on his way to work—and feeds them Tums! And the butlers and maids from some of the fashionable Seacliff dwellings strolling hand in hand down shaded, out-of-the-way lanes—discreet, even on their afternoons off.

Lazing ex-servicemen, putting their discarded GI clothing to good Sunday use—pink pants, leather flying jackets, GI shoes, mixed incongruously with loud civilian adornments in a final, all-out expression of contempt for regimentation. The somewhat amusing "excursion boat" that floats sightseers around tiny Stow Lake—which is a little like taking a sightseeing tour in your own back yard. Ralph Murray leading his Park Band through "The Whistler and His Dog"—and

181

you listen to the familiar chirpy theme and dreamily realize that here in the heart of the Park time almost stands still on a sunny Sunday. Plundering sea gulls, desert their Bayliwick to sweep down on the tiny lakes and snatch away donations of bread from the polite and cloistered ducks, who, never having ventured into the Outside World, seem almost wounded by such ferocious hunger.

The policeman's horse, standing handsomely at attention while his not-so-handsome rider dismounts to lend a hand at directing the traffic of this horseless age. An old couple in the Japanese Tea Garden watching a young couple ride by on a bicycle built for two, and turning to each other to smile: "Remember when we . . ." and that is all, for what more was there to say? A young army pilot, drawing smiles in Steinhart Aquarium by drawling over and over, as he watched the sharks streaking back and forth, "Ah jes' cain't get over it—they got fins just like a B-29, yessir, just like a B-29!" Soldiers and sailors, who must have had their fill of standing in line by this time, patiently waiting in long queues for bicycles, for horses, for boats. And the oblivious couples who unashamedly make love on the grassy banks and knolls—lost to the world in each other.

And then the sudden sensation of returning to reality that hits you as you roll out of the Park and get caught up in the hectic swirl of traffic at the Beach.

The huge souvenir and gadget emporium next to the Cliff House—where the great plate-glass windows open out on one of the greatest sights in the world; where, free for nothing, you can see a super-panorama of sea and sky, of bridge and harbor, of ships at the end of their voyage home (yet, right next to the window unseeing guys and gals line up to drop their nickels in a trick picture machine that shows Sally Rand doing her Fan Dance!).

This is a Sunday at the Park—a pageant of little children and big children getting lost with each other in the heart of a city, each knowing deep down inside that there's always tomorrow, and that tomorrow is always Monday.

28.

THESE FOOLISH THINGS

San Francisco, brought to life by the lusty, gusty roars of the gold seekers, has never taken itself too seriously. From the very start there has been life and laughter in Baghdad-by-the-Bay, with every citizen a potential comedian, every stuffed shirt the inevitable butt of a joke, every facet of the city's life wide open to the snide observation.

One of the earliest recorded instances of civic humor occurred one night in the 1850s, during a performance of *The Hunchback* at the American Theatre. During a fight scene between two of the leading actors, a third thespian strode onto the stage, threw out both arms, and shouted: "What does this mean?"

To a man the gallery roared back: "Sidewheel steamer!" and the entire theater, cast and all, burst into a hubbub of laughter.

(Explanation for late-comers: At that time a semaphore that signaled the coming of ships through the Golden Gate stood atop Telegraph Hill. When the arms of the semaphore were horizontal, it announced the arrival of a Pacific Mail sidewheel steamer.)

One of San Francisco's most venerable landmarks is a Clay Street restaurant called Tadich's Grill, subtitled in gold letters on its front window: "The Original Cold Day Restaurant." A fairly confusing legend, that, until you learn that some sixty years ago it was the favorite hangout of a politician named Alexander Badlam, who used to boast loudly and apparently endlessly: "It'll be a cold day when they beat *me* at the polls!"

Although the restaurant continues to immortalize that statement, the Badlam legend wound up as you might expect —with an inevitable resounding defeat in a city election. The next morning, early, a messenger rapped on the door of his Franklin Street mansion and silently handed him two blankets and a bearskin rug. A few minutes later a wagon arrived and dumped a ton of coal on his front sidewalk. And every day for weeks thereafter an iceman deposited one hundred pounds of ice on his porch, while gleeful neighbors peered out from behind their lace curtains and tittered.

It was as a young man in pre-fire San Francisco that the unforgettable Gelett Burgess wrote his "Purple Cow" quatrain (you know, "I'd rather see than be one") and recited it over and over in pubs, to the delight of hangers-on. The deathless verse was first published in *The Lark*, the city's

185

long-gone magazine for the literati, and then raced across the nation on grateful tongues.

But what few people remember is that in a subsequent issue of *The Lark*, published two or three months later, appeared another quatrain by Burgess, which went, with a clearly audible sigh, like this:

> Oh yes, I wrote the "Purple Cow,"
> I'm sorry now I wrote it;
> But I can tell you anyhow,
> I'll kill you if you quote it!

Even the catastrophe of April 18, 1906, was not without its moments of memorable humor. While militant moralists were preaching that a wrathful God had shaken the wicked city and applied the torch, the irrepressible Charlie Field noticed that Hotaling's whisky warehouse still stood intact in the middle of an otherwise razed business district, and jingled gaily:

> If, as they say, God spanked the town
> For being over-frisky;
> Why did He burn the churches down
> And spare Hotaling's whisky?

At the end of World War I, in an attempt to halt a flu epidemic that was sweeping the city, health officials distributed white gauze masks to practically every San Franciscan. Then came the news of the Armistice, and, joyously defying orders, the men ripped off their masks and dashed into the nearest drinking place. It was at this festive moment that an unidentified Market Street wit observed happily: "Thank God I've

186

lived to see the day when the churches are closed, the saloons open, and the women muzzled!"

The volunteer gagsters who keep a columnist in business are tireless. In spite of hellish prices and high taxes, they somehow find time to mail in their observations-on-post-card. A favorite subject is the transportation system. It was Jerry Bundsen who first thought of calling the Municipal Railway the "Muniserable Railway." And because James Turner is the nominal boss of this city-owned transit system, it didn't take Arthur Caylor long to dub the ancient streetcars "Turnerville Trolleys." On the other hand, Howard Young found something laudable about the cars. "At least they rattle before they strike," he pointed out. But another contributor, tired of being squeezed into the overcrowded busses and trolleys, wanted to know whether the slogan of the Public Utilities Commission was "The Public Be Jammed!"

Even the Southern Pacific commute trains that serve the Peninsula suburbs fail to escape the sardonic wrath of their customers. Most of the names they call the trains are unprintable, but a commuter named Paul Speegle hit on one that has stuck (and in the Southern Pacific's craw too). He calls his particular rattler "The 19th Century Limited."

San Francisco's maddening midtown complex of one-way streets, dead-end alleys, and intersections marked "No Right Turn—No Left Turn," add up to a certain hysterical kind of humor too. For instance, there was the plight of the touring motorist who stopped at Fifth and Mission streets to ask Officer John Gehring how to get to a certain address in the heart of the financial district, on the other side of horrendous Market Street.

"Well, let's see," began John, looking north along Mission, "you can go down that way about two blocks, and—nope, nope, can't turn there." He faced south, with a faraway look in his eyes. "Go up this way to the corner after next and—hm. Can't cross Market there." He stopped, reached a hand up under his cap, and finally shrugged. "I'm sorry, mister. I guess there's just *no* way to get there from here!"

There has been much hullabaloo lately about building a second Bay Bridge, the first one being incapable of handling the tremendous daily flow of traffic between San Francisco and the East Bay. Most San Franciscans and the four daily newspapers have been hoping that the second bridge would be built far to the south of the present span, but Governor Earl Warren and the California Toll Bridge Authority stubbornly approved a parallel bridge.

The "twin bridge," they call it. But cynical San Franciscans immediately substituted their own name—the "double cross."

Laughs are usually available backstage at the magnificent War Memorial Opera House. I'll never forget the night Lily Pons refused to go on until a stagehand had sprayed the atmosphere with a Flit gun filled with Chanel No. 5. Or the time the actor dressed as the bear for *La Bohème* kept wandering around the stage long after he should have been off, whereupon the director shouted from the wings, in a stage "whisper" that could be heard to the topmost seat in the balcony, "Get that goddam bear off the stage!"

A San Francisco operatic hero for a short time was a state highway patrolman named George Stinson, who possessed a fine tenor voice and was widely publicized as, of course, "The Singing Cop." Between his long, hard hours on a state motorcycle Stinson studied diligently and was at last given the tenor role in *Pagliacci.*

As he was standing nervously in the wings waiting to make his debut before a packed Opera House, he was approached by Impresario Gaetano Merola, who said: "George, you look fine, wonderful. Except for one thing. I think you have too much white make-up on."

"That's not make-up," groaned George. "That's *me!*"

One night during the 1946 season Maestro Merola wanted Tenor Jan Peerce to sing the lead in *La Bohème,* but Peerce refused because that night happened to be Rosh Hashana, the Jewish New Year. Argued Merola valiantly: "Look, Jan. New York is your home. With daylight saving, there's four hours' difference between New York and San Francisco. So—we start the performance at eight fifteen, and by you, Rosh Hashana is over at home."

"Sorry," returned Peerce implacably. "Rosh Hashana is where you find it."

Then we have the inveterate punster. Such a one is John Cary Lucas, a denizen of the financial district, who pulled the most bodacious pun of 1949. It was inspired when the Mechanics Institute on Post Street attempted to close its foyer clubroom, the headquarters of some one hundred and fifty old-time chess players. The room is "bedraggled," said the trustees of the Institute. Some of the chess players look "seedy." And "their coming and going reflects on the Institute's dignity."

Lucas, however, had no sympathy with the Institute's viewpoint. Said he indignantly: "They're just trying to pull their chess nuts out of the foyer."

A magazine writer named Franc Shor won fleeting fame when he referred to a landlord who owns a decrepit duplex on Telegraph Hill as "The Lessor of Two Evils." And the Sunset District, a section of tiny white all-alike stucco houses built by a contractor named Henry Doelger received its most amusing description from an unidentified punster who called it simply "The White Cliffs of Doelger."

The endless subject of weather and climate always brings out the best and worst in the San Franciscan. On Grant Avenue one afternoon I overheard a stout matron telling a stranger about the "perfect" San Francisco climate. "It's so *even*," she enthused. "The temperature is practically the same all day and all night. Why, sometimes the maximum is even lower than the minimum!"

During a cocktail party the chatter drifted around to a familiar subject—The Best Place to Live—and a visiting New Yorker remarked typically: "As far as I'm concerned, there's no place as lovely as New York in October."

THESE FOOLISH THINGS

Quietly cut in Edith MacInnis: "It's *always* October—in San Francisco."

Which reminds me that I've been an ardent admirer of Kathryn Grayson, the singing screen star, ever since she made her first visit to New York City and pulled one of the all-time great switches. Asked during a press interview whether she liked The Big Town, she smiled: "Yes, indeed. It reminds me so much of San Francisco!"

One of the neatest phrases ever turned out about the city was manufactured at Jack's one lunchtime by Marcus Sieff, young president of a chain of mercantile stores in Britain. Introduced to a man who wondered whether he was in San Francisco on business or pleasure, Sieff replied: "It's always a pleasure to be in San Franscisco—on business."

A perennial fan of San Francisco is Dudley Field Malone, the noted barrister who was Assistant Secretary of State under Woodrow Wilson and was once Collector of the Port of New York. After living in or near the city for years, Malone moved to Arizona, and in Phoenix one day he ran into a visiting San Franciscan named Alex Haas, who wondered: "What are you doing down here? Not ill, are you?"

"Yes," nodded Malone with a wistful smile. "I've got heart trouble. You see, my doctor says I have to live in Arizona— and my heart is still in San Francisco."

On the other hand, there is the problem of visiting Los Angelenos—such as a Southlandish character named Ben Martin who cornered me on Market Street one day, talked innocently of this and that, and then inquired: "By the way, when was the earthquake that ruined this town?"

"If you mean the fire," I said testily, "it was in 1906."

He looked around for a few seconds (knew he had me trapped), and then sugared sweetly: "Isn't it about time they started rebuilding?"

If I'd been real quick, I wouldn't have stood there with my mouth opening and closing wordlessly, like a fish. I'd have reminded him of the time the Los Angeles Police Department was ordered by a blue-nosed district attorney to confiscate all copies of *Lysistrata*.

A conscientious, clean-minded police captain went one step further. He sent out a detail to arrest the author.

But my favorite little tales are the ones that just sort of evolve naturally and logically—on the streets, in the eating places, at the bars.

I remember the recent fine morning when City Supervisor Marvin Lewis and Merchant Cyril Magnin, walking down to work, decided to stop in at Compton's cafeteria on Geary Street for a quick cup of coffee. At the next table, busily engrossed in ham and eggs, sat Governor Earl Warren.

"Hello, Mr. Governor," smiled Lewis.

"Good morning, Mr. Supervisor," nodded Warren.

"By the way, Governor," went on Lewis, "I'd like you to meet Cyril Magnin—he owns the Joseph Magnin stores."

At this point a Compton habitué, a typical member of cafeteria society, growled in disgust, clapped on his hat, and started for the door, observing loudly: "Yaaah, Mr. Governor, Mr. Supervisor, Mr. Magnin! Everybody's nuts around here this morning!"

THESE FOOLISH THINGS

Some time before Pearl Harbor, Kathleen Norris, the evergreen novelist, was an ardent member of "America First," the militant anti-intervention group. So when Charles Lindbergh, a leader of the group, arrived in San Francisco, it was only logical that she should invite him down to her Palo Alto mansion for a Sunday of brunching and swimming.

Lindbergh turned out to be an excellent swimmer. He was especially adept at swimming under water, and the guests stood by the pool enthralled as he raced the length of the pool several times without coming up for air.

"An amazing man, Lindbergh," loudly observed Fred Thompson, Mrs. Norris's brother. "He's great in the air. He's great under water. But on dry land—he ain't so good!"

Thompson, incidentally, lives in Marin County, and one day he picked up a Filipino hitchhiker, a neighboring farmer, and drove him into San Francisco. As they reached their destination, the Filipino began an effusive speech of thanks, loud and long. Fred waved airily. "Forget it. Don't mention it."

The Filipino bent over confidentially and whispered: "O.K., Mr. Thompson, I won't. I won't mention it to a soul."

There are usually a few smiles around the hotels too.

For instance, Dave Falk, a ranking member of café society, lived for a long time at the Fairmont Hotel, and noticed one night that the contents of a fine bottle of bourbon seemed to be mysteriously below the level of the night before. So, suspecting the chambermaid, he made a tiny pencil mark on the label opposite the whisky. The next night, when he returned home, he found a note from the maid. It read: "Please don't put a

193

pencil mark on the bottle, because I don't want to put water in such good bourbon."

The main-floor bar of the Mark Hopkins for years has been the unofficial headquarters for the drinking members of the fashionable younger set. Especially the young ladies. Their babblings, their preenings, and their posturings always defied description (mine, at least) until the night the prominent Mrs. Roy Pike walked in, surveyed the scene, and summed it all up. "It could be worse," she said after a moment's reflection. "After all, just think what wonderful wives they'll make their second husbands!"

A couple of years ago the Mark ran a series of newspaper and billboard advertisements reading: "Cook's Night Out—a very special dinner served Thursdays from 6 P.M. in the Grill." A few weeks later Hart Smith, assistant manager of the hotel, received in the mail a copy of that ad, plus this note from a Pacific Heights matron: "Your ad is very convincing. Our cook now eats at the Mark every Thursday night."

Dan London, general manager of Hotel St. Francis, is a man who overlooks no bets. One of his chambermaids walked into Screenstar Hedy Lamarr's suite and found the mattress, sheets, and blankets on the floor—a minor mystery that Hedy explained simply enough: "The bed in this room squeaks so loudly I couldn't fall asleep. So—I slept on the floor." Mr. London immediately ordered a small sign affixed to the carpet for a couple of days. It read: "Hedy Lamarr Slept Here."

It was in the lobby of the St. Francis that I overheard a memorable conversation between the wife of a San Francisco labor leader and a prominent clubwoman who had just met for the first time, lunched together, and apparently had got along famously. As they parted, Mrs. Labor Leader declared warmly: "We must have lunch again. Frankly, I've always been a little afraid of you, but now that we've met, I find you're just as common as I am!"

Cabdrivers, strip teasers, artists, bartenders—they all have something important to say or do, if you just happen to be around at the right time.

Ted Galanter, who represents Louis B. Mayer in San Francisco, stepped into a cab in front of the Fairmont with a couple of slightly overdressed Hollywood celebrities—whereupon the cabby looked them over balefully, slid behind the wheel, and mumbled to nobody in general: "Characters, *always* characters. Never people!"

John Grace, an architect who lives in Mill Valley, went to a psychiatrist for an examination, and was warmly greeted by the doctor's receptionist, who had known him for a long time.

"Well, John," she greeted, "you look fine after all these years. But why the beard and beret?"

"That," solemnly returned Grace, "is what I am here to find out."

For years one of my favorite characters (characters, always characters) was a redheaded strip-tease artist named "Frenchy," who worked, with considerable zeal showing, in a Mason Street spot called The Streets of Paris. "Frenchy" was a cut above the usual stripteuse in mental as well as physical capacities. Two of her fondest admirers for a while were William Saroyan, the writer, and handsome Prince Franzi von Hohenlohe, son of that mysterious prewar friend of Adolf Hitler known as Princess Stephanie von Hohenlohe.

"Frenchy" never played her favorite trick on them. But she used it with unfailing success on the twenty or thirty "wolves" who'd bother her for a date in the course of an evening. To each of them she'd confide: "Well, my boy friend is in Sacramento tonight, so maybe it'll be O.K. Tellya what, gimme a buck so I can call him up and see whether he's coming back."

The answer, of course, was always "Sorry, he'll be here tonight."

(What "Frenchy" didn't know was that she was pulling a switch on a hoary practice that flourished during the short days and long nights of the old Barbary Coast. Some of the wiser dance-hall girls used to sell "the" key to their room to eager swains for $5.00—only the key never fitted the lock, and the girl wasn't there anyway.)

Oh yes, characters aplenty. John Coulthard, a commercial artist of note, ran into an unusual type recently: a complete stranger who walked unannounced into his penthouse studio in the Mutual Building. "Do you mind if I look out of your window?" he asked Coulthard, who could think of nothing more incisive than a blank shake of his head.

The stranger then walked over to the window and looked out silently for a few minutes, nodding now and then to himself as though in great satisfaction. As he walked out, he tipped his hat and said "Thanks very much." At the door he suddenly stopped and smiled to the mystified Coulthard: "Oh, I forgot to tell you. My hobby is collecting views."

Another character who keeps scampering through my mind is Bob McIntyre, an ex-pugilist who eventually wound up running a cafeteria on Turk Street. Once upon a long time ago Bob was matched for a San Francisco fight against a cream-puff puncher named Sailor Hughes. McIntyre won easily, and after the decision had been announced, he swaggered over to the sailor's corner, pulled a peanut out of his mouth, and sneered: "Hughes, you're a bum. Why don'tcha give up? See this here peanut? I put in in me mouth before the foist round, I had it there all through the fight—and look, it ain't even cracked!"

Sailor Hughes got red in the face. "So," he roared, "ya t'ink I ain't got no stren'th, huh?" With which he grabbed the peanut out of McIntyre's hand and smashed it with one blow.

For the past ten years—I claim the distinction of having "discovered" him—a favorite San Francisco personality has been a youngish, dapperish bar waiter named Johnny Williams. Williams is just like any other bar waiter except for one small difference: he drives to and from work in a limousine driven by a liveried chauffeur.

This, you'll admit, is at least a whimsical approach to the business of waiting on people. And the chauffeured limousine is no part-time, rental-by-the-hour gimmick, either. Both the car and the driver are his—and please don't ask me how he manages to pay for them. I've asked him many times, as have hundreds of other San Franciscans, and his only reply is an inscrutable smile, accompanied by the polite fluff-off: "Pardon me, did you say you wanted that scotch with soda—or water?"

Although he doesn't talk much, Williams is occasionally capable of an amusing observation. A few years ago he lost his job as waiter in a Mason Street saloon, and that night I found him lounging against the bar with a troubled look on his face.

"I just can't make up my mind," he said, staring into his champagne cocktail. "I don't know whether to fire my chauffeur—or apply for my unemployment insurance!"

Because of the widespread publicity he inevitably received, Williams attracted a lot of attention and admirers, one of whom sent him a live rabbit at Easter. "Of course," he said, stroking it gently, "I'm going to give this away."

"That's nice," I said. "To a kid?"

"No," he replied gravely. "To another rabbit."

World War II stopped Johnny Williams' career as a character. He served with distinction in the Pacific with the Marines, and at last word was managing the cocktail lounge in San Francisco's handsome Marine Memorial Building. He has given up his limousine and chauffeur in favor of a more lavish hobby, befitting his higher station in life. Now he is buying race horses.

Along San Franscisco's troubled water front Harry Bridges isn't the only man with the smart cracks. During the 1946 crisis (every year brings a crisis to the harbor) the Government appointed a three-man fact-finding board to look into the problem. The board's first problem was one of its own: should it hold its sessions in San Francisco or Washington?

Chairman James L. Fly eventually swung the balance in favor of San Francisco. "We should be there to find out what really goes on along the water front," he explained. "Besides, I don't want to go on thinking that a winch is a disreputable woman."

Bridges' chief and dearly-unbeloved rival along the water front is a big, peanut-nosed individual named Harry Lundeberg, president of the Sailors Union of the Pacific, who is just as salty as his CIO opposite number. At a meeting of a steamshippers' organization called the Propellor Club last year Lundeberg was asked to pose for a picture standing next to Lewis Lapham, president of the American-Hawaiian Steamship Company.

Lundeberg didn't say a word to Lapham. He merely looked him up and down for a few silent seconds in a somewhat perplexed manner. Finally he grunted to the mystified Lapham: "Cripes but you're thin for a shipowner!"

San Francisco's amateur humorists overlook nothing. When "the world's finest underground garage" was built beneath historic Union Square in the heart of the city, a contributor named Martha Snow sat right down and composed this:

> The little park that wasn't there
> Was formerly called Union Square;
> But now it has a third dimension,
> So "Union Cube" is our suggestion.

When the results of a city election were published one day, the great attorney, the late Gavin McNab scanned the list of new supervisors and predicted classically: "On the day these men take office, every burglar alarm in town will go off automatically."

When the picturesque little Marin County town of Sausalito became the haven for scores of British refugees, just before World War II, Ted Courtney looked over the scene sourly and observed: "This town is getting overloaded with tweedy bags in baggy tweeds."

When Mel Threlkeld, an advertising agency executive, returned to his Belvedere home one day last year he found a chair smoldering away, so quicklike he telephoned the Belvedere Fire Department and hollered for the chief. "Sorry," said the girl who answered the phone, "but the chief is out. Uh—is it anything important?"

"That," drawled Threlkeld, "all depends on whether he wants a small fire now or a big fire later."

When it was a favorite parlor diversion to make up definitions of liberals, radicals, communists, et cetera, Max Radin, then a professor of law at University of California, achieved this deathless definition of a liberal: "A radical with a wife and child." You've heard it before? Radin said it first.

It was Radin, incidentally, who told me this story about a colleague of his. Perhaps it's the absent-minded professor story to end them all, and high time. Anyway, this savant awoke one Saturday morning with the shocked realization that he'd had a dinner date at a lady's house the preceding Wednesday night.

THESE FOOLISH THINGS

Without even pausing to brush his orange juice or drink his teeth, he dashed to the telephone, called her, and gurgled breathlessly: "My dear, I want to apologize. About Wednesday night—you must forgive me. I just can't imagine how I could have forgotten it. Now please say you'll give me another chance."

There was a stony silence on the other end, broken at last by her cold voice: "I don't know what you're apologizing about. You were *here* Wednesday night."

Even great, gray San Quentin, one of the largest prisons in the world (pop.: 5000) produces its per-capita quotient of smiles. I've seen few sights more sardonic than that of a young prisoner walking through the yard with an Army Good Conduct ribbon pinned to his prison cap. One day, in that same yard, I watched a life-termer maneuver for fully five minutes to keep a black cat from crossing his path. It was in that yard that a prisoner named O'Brien looked at a guard and sneered deliciously: "There, but for the grace of God, go I!"

In 1939, shortly after Tom Mooney had been freed by Governor Olson amid much fanfare, I asked Dr. Leo Stanley, San Quentin's chief surgeon, if he'd care to name Mooney's successor as the prison's "most famous" inmate.

"I guess it's Frank Egan," said the doc after giving the question considerable thought. "But," he added sniffishly, glancing over at Alcatraz shimmering in the middle of the Bay, "we don't use the star system—like certain other prisons."

This isn't the kind of conversation you would normally over-hear on busy Powell Street, between Ellis and O'Farrell, but that's where it happened, and I heard it.

A bakery wagon drove up to a restaurant, and as the driver began unloading cookies, he noticed a little Negro boy, about five, staring at him with mouth-watery eyes. "Hi, kid," said the driver pleasantly. "What's your name?"

"Jimmy," was the answer, and the driver grinned. "Well, well, that's *my* name too. Just for that, here's a cookie."

The moppet munched for a second, and then piped up: "Mister, kin I have a cookie for my brother too?"

"Oh, I dunno," smiled the driver. "What's *his* name?"

"Jimmy," said the kid.

On the other hand, an example of the abysmal ignorance of the younger generation. A short time ago Attorneys Vincent Hallinan, James Martin MacInnis, and Archer Zamloch moved their offices into a remodeled old house on Franklin Street, and began looking around for furnishings and decorations in authentic "Gay Nineties" style. To help them out, a friend named Maurice Moskovitz presented them with a handsome gift—a pre-1906 brass cuspidor, huge and highly polished.

As he set it down on the front desk, Receptionist Marie Coughlin, aged twenty-five, looked admiringly at it and gushed: "Gee, Mr. Moskovitz, what a perfectly *gorgeous* fruit bowl!"

Shortly after Congress first refused to lift the OPA restrictions on rentals, a small but indignant meeting of certain landlords took place in San Francisco. As they sputtered around for a way of properly expressing their outraged sensibilities, a landlord arose to propose that they all paint their buildings funereal black.

"That," he insisted, "will show Congress that our chances of making an honest buck are dead."

Another landlord promptly suggested that black wasn't subtle enough. "What we should do," he said, "is show 'em what we think of their socialistic nonsense by painting our buildings red."

As this clever ruse was being discussed, a little old lady who owns a couple of small apartment houses (stories like this always have Little Old Ladies) sang out timidly: "Why not paint them all yellow?"

There was a moment's silence, and then the chairman smiled. "Maybe I'm dull, but just what would the color yellow signify?"

"I don't know," admitted the little old lady. "I just like yellow."

At the San Francisco Press Club one night a politico named Mort Donaghue, relaxing over a newspaper at the bar, happened to read a dispatch stating that Pope Pius XII was ill, a bit of information that, at the time and place, somehow hit Brother Donaghue rather forcibly. So he picked up the telephone and asked the long-distance operator to get him the Vatican.

After a reasonable delay Mort was connected with a Father Murphy of the Vatican staff in Rome, who said: "Very nice of you to call, Mr. Donaghue, and His Holiness is feeling much better, thank you. By the way, where did you say you were calling from?"

"San Francisco, California," said Donaghue, whereupon the priest returned: " Well, if it isn't too much trouble, would you mind calling my brother in Reno, Nevada, and giving him my greetings?"

"Glad to," said Mort, and a few minutes later he located Father Murphy's brother, who's in the used-car business in Reno.

"Hello," greeted Donaghue. "I'm calling from San Francisco. I just talked to your brother in the Vatican and he asked me to call you and give you his regards."

"Well!" remarked the voice in Reno. "I'll be damned!"

Saloons, of course, are an ideal watering place for incidents that are memorable, amusing, and even ridiculous.

During the war, when every bar in San Francisco was making a small fortune at the expense of outgoing, hang-the-price servicemen, a musician was lucky enough to buy a small joint on Market Street. He acted as his own bartender, and for three solid years cleaned up on the soldiers and sailors who, understandably enough, acted as though each drink were their last.

One day near the end of the war an old-hand bartender named Rudy Perez dropped in to say hello to this unlovable character. As they were chatting, a young sailor walked up to the bar and asked for a Tom Collins.

THESE FOOLISH THINGS

The ex-musician grabbed a glass, threw some ice, lemon juice, and a cherry into it, filled it to the top with seltzer water, and handed it to the sailor—who promptly downed the drink, smacked his lips, threw down a fifty-cent piece, and walked out.

After the sailor had gone, Perez leaned over to the ex-musician and said: "I know it's none of my business—but how come you didn't put any gin in that Collins?"

A look of genuine amazement spread over the ex-musician's face. "You put *gin* in a Tom Collins?" he asked incredulously.

For three years he had been serving lemonade as Tom Collinses at fifty cents a throw, and not once had he received a complaint. Psychology?

Another bartender (we'll call him Joe) was involved one night in an incident he'll never forget. He was working behind the bar in a North Beach saloon when a customer began getting loud and obstreperous. So the owner of the place signaled Joe to give the customer a "Mickey Finn." (If you've never been associated with a "Mickey," consider yourself lucky. It's an undetectable white powder that, dissolved in a drink, has an immediate and distressing effect on the consumer.)

Surreptitiously, he thought, Joe slipped the powder into the noisy customer's next scotch. But—the customer saw him. Grabbing Joe by his lapels, the intended victim dragged him halfway across the bar and snarled:

"I saw that, wise guy. And now I'll tell you what we're gonna do. You and me and the boss are gonna play a new kind of 'Russian Roulette.' You mix him a scotch, and mix yourself a scotch, and put that drink with the Mickey on the bar. Then we're gonna move the three glasses around and around on the bar—and when I yell 'Drink!' we pick up the nearest glass and drink, see?"

For minutes that seemed endless the three men moved the glasses around in a circle. "Drink!" shouted the customer. "Just a minute," cut in the white-faced Joe. "Do you mind, sir, if I move the glasses around once more?" No objection. They drank. Then they stood there glaring at one another.

A few seconds later Joe snapped to attention, bravely gasped: "We who are about to die salute you!" and ran for the door.

But my favorite bartender story happened in a place called The House That Jack Built, on Broadway in North Beach. In walked a man who ordered a straight shot of whisky, gulped it down, ordered another straight shot, drank that, and then laid a dollar bill on the bar and walked out.

"Can you imagine a guy like that?" mused the bartender, sticking the dollar into his pocket. "He has two drinks, leaves a dollar tip, and then walks out without paying!"

But, as I observed earlier in this chapter, it's the tourists that a San Franciscan has to watch out for.

Sergeant Ed Moore of the Golden Gate Bridge staff, whose hobby is collecting true tales about his customers, tells about the tourist from New York who drove across the mighty span, turned around at the other end, drove back to the tollgate, and spat at Ed:

THESE FOOLISH THINGS

"Fer gosh sakes—is *that* all there is to the damn thing?"

This, to a San Franciscan's native pride, was almost as disastrous as the day Stock Broker Henry Manheim took a pair of visiting Chicagoans out to the Beach for their first glimpse of the Pacific Ocean.

After staring out across the water for a few moments, one of the Midwesterners turned to the other and shrugged: "Hm. It's not as big as I thought it would be!"

29.

WHAT IS SAN FRANCISCO?

This is no exaggeration: The San Franciscan can get homesick for his own city—without leaving it.

I've experienced this rather unusual sensation. Working downtown, I've sometimes felt such an overpowering urge to see Golden Gate Park that I've had to stop everything, jump in my car, and drive out there. It seemed as though I hadn't visited the place for years. It was like returning to a long-forgotten world, a thousand miles and a million memories away.

I've had people in the Mission District tell me that one Sunday they suddenly decided to pack a lunch and ride a streetcar crosstown to the Marina, for a picnic on the greensward alongside Yacht Harbor. It was more than just a Sunday outing. They felt—and they tried to describe the feeling to me—that they were on a trip to another place that they had always loved and continually wanted to see again.

WHAT IS SAN FRANCISCO?

I suppose the explanation for all this is logical enough—and yet peculiarly San Franciscan. It's because there is such infinite variety in the patchwork of the city. It's because "San Francisco"—the definition thereof—is so many different things to so many different people. That's why the city is full of wanderers within its own boundaries, each feeling a "pull" toward the particular facet that, to him, answers the question:

"What is San Francisco?"

It's the noon siren in the half-dead Ferry Building, sounding off ferociously each day as though to convince itself and all San Francisco that it's still an integral part of Baghdad-by-the-Bay. It's Lefty O'Doul on the side lines at Seals Stadium, talking pep talk to his players and shouting small talk to his pals in the stands. It's the fog that sweeps in suddenly at the end of a sun-kissed day to blot out the Russ Building and her sister spires in a swirl of atomic mist. And it's the tiny stores along Columbus Avenue, where a strange and wondrous combination of Italian, Chinese, Spanish, and English is spoken by the customers, all adding up to a harmony that might well be studied by Trygve Lie and associates.

Yes, that's San Francisco—to some. To others, it's the Palace's Happy Valley bar at noon, jammed with businessmen who drink their lunches and get ulcers at the job of being successful. It's the Sunset District shopping district at 10 A.M., alive with cute young Doelgerized housewives in slacks, pushing baby carriages with one hand and preening their permanents with the other. It's the pageants of transportation you see from Telegraph Hill—the Belt Line railroad inching along, trucks rattling around the Embarcadero, ships poking their noses into piers, aircraft making tiny marks in the sky.

That's San Francisco—and yet it isn't. Because it's also the mellow charm of the Sunday-afternoon band concerts in Golden Gate Park, where the people relax in the sun and listen to waltzes that will never die, and little kids roll around on the lawn, and bareheaded, baldheaded oldsters puff thoughtfully on their cigars, and the women cling to their men and close their eyes, and the year could be 1895 or 1910 or 1923—anything but the year it is.

And it's the always amazing experience of rounding a Twin Peaks curve and coming upon row after row of white houses, all built by a super contractor, all the same, all joined together like long barracks, all undulating over hills that were once green and fresh and natural.

And it's the sensuous swell of San Francisco that you see as you head home across the Golden Gate Bridge—a rising and falling of concrete waves tinted golden brown by the setting sun. And the weird out-of-this-worldliness you always feel as you enter Top o' the Mark to sit in the dim light by a vast window, looking out on a view that seems as phony as a stage set. And the monumental untidiness of Market Street— a never-ending eyesore of scraps and trash and hokum and junk, mixed unceremoniously with fine stores and venerable buildings to form a blatant symphony of discords.

It's the unidentifiable "municipal" smell inside the City

Hall, a smell that somehow springs out of all public buildings, an odor that your nose remembers from your days in school—a combination of paper and paste pots and pencil sharpeners and body odor and the blood of taxpayers. And it's the collection of Same Old Faces that you always see in certain places, an eternal verity that breeds confidence and well-being and seems substantial in a world coming apart at the seams; like the Harrison Kolbs at a Curran opening night, and E. Pym Jones applauding Hildegarde at the Mark, and Hartley Peart lunching at the Palace, and Joe the Doorman opening limousine doors outside of Shreve's jewelry store.

That is some of San Francisco. That, plus a thousand other things, blended in with the mixed-up moods of the city—the old landmarks and the brave new plans, the battered traditions and the newcomers that never heard of them, the familiar hills and the unfamiliar problems that dwarf them. And always the Bay, always the restless fog, always the people running around as though they knew what they were doing—but always glad they're doing it in San Francisco.

30.

WHY I LIKE SAN FRANCISCO

Some time ago the magazine *Pageant* asked me to answer the simple but difficult question: "Why do you live in San Francisco?"

Instead of trying to flip off an immediate answer, I put the same question to a lot of acquaintances around town. Some of them just stared back at me blankly, their manner indicating clearly that they considered it a stupid question. Where else, for Heaven's sake, would anyone want to live?

Others shrugged and made offhand references to "the scenery—I never get tired of looking at it," and some said "the weather agrees with me," and a few sacrilegious ones just didn't know because they had never had the chance to go anywhere else anyway.

Despite the above confusion, it's not quite true to say that everybody has a different reason for living in San Fran-

WHY I LIKE SAN FRANCISCO

cisco. In fact, *Pageant,* in presenting my answers, asked a supposedly rhetorical question of its own: "Ever see a San Franciscan who was not in love with his city?" I've met a few, but they state their objections in a discreetly low tone of voice. Otherwise, they're a cinch to get that "Why don'tcha go back where you came from?" treatment even faster than "foreigners" who might point out that some things are better in the Old Country.

The average San Franciscan, if I may presume to identify myself as one, is a notoriously smug character. Visitors, especially from Los Angeles, are quick to point this out, especially after they've received the usual needling remarks about the Colossus of the South. San Franciscans won't deny the charge, either. "Smug, smog, what's the difference?" they'll reply, "Except that you have the smog." *Touché!*

This very smugness is a peculiarly satisfying part of the civic pride that still burns strongly among San Franciscans. It's nice to be part of a city that is proud of itself, a city that carries itself straight and tall on the slopes of its hills, the better to gaze fondly over its own charms. It's nice to belong to a sort of mutual-admiration society, whose members silently congratulate one another daily for having had the wisdom and foresight to settle in this best of all possible cities. I don't imagine for a minute that the average Podunkian grabs the hand of his neighbor every now and then and says: "Lucky you, to be living in Podunk."

To revert to the personal, I like the looks of the city I call home. The imposing bristle of skyscrapers in the financial district, built on land that was once water—to me, they're arranged just so in just the right place, to look like a city should look. The gray fingers of the fog, stealing over Twin Peaks or pausing for a rest on the Marin hilltops—I like the frosty, frozen fillip they add to an otherwise sunswept panorama. The hilly streets that are reached by wooden stairs, the prohibition-flavored saloons at the end of dark alleys, the orange lights of the Bay Bridge mirrored on the midnight waters of the Bay—these I love, for each proclaims to me, every day, that San Franscisco is, in the truest sense of that overworked word, "different."

For a city that is comparatively small, San Francisco keeps presenting an exciting challenge to exploration, even to those who've lived in it all their lives. It is a place of many worlds, one blending into the other without losing its character. Perhaps a single street—Grant Avenue—will explain what I mean.

Starting at Market Street, Grant Avenue begins its life in a richly perfumed atmosphere of fine shops, banks, sidewalk flower stands, and clicking high heels echoing the expensive click of limousine doors opened and closed by bowing doormen. This is Grant Avenue, a world of refined finery—and yet it is not. Step across one street—Bush—and in a matter of seconds you're in Chinatown.

Grant Avenue is the main street of the section so dearly beloved by the Chamber of Commerce—where even the street lamps are festooned with gilded dragons and the shopwindows are loaded with the treasures and trifles of another culture, and the tourist can do no wrong except to go away empty-handed. Grant Avenue is "Chinatown" to the visitor, who seldom ventures into the tiny, back-alley restaurants where the cooks never heard of chop suey—but can do wonderful things with a duck that is inflated like an automobile tire and glazed until it resembles a ceramic, and yet turns out to be as strange and wonderful to the palate as a Ming vase is to the eye.

But Grant Avenue isn't Chinatown, either. From the corner where you stopped to watch two ancient Chinese playing mah-jongg, you step onto another corner—just across the street, literally—to kibitz a wild-armed conversation between two Italians who became good Americans without ever learning to speak English.

And still Grant Avenue draws you on, through "Little Italy" and into what is left of San Francisco's Bohemia, the tiny wooden houses of the painters and the writers and the sculptors on the slopes of Telegraph Hill, where you half-expect to see Jack London walking down the street, his long, curly hair flowing in the breeze from the Bay that is now in full sight.

You still ask, "Why do I like San Francisco?"

Because Grant Avenue isn't unique. It's typical.

The San Franciscan, whether he realizes it or not, lives a pretty exciting life. He has one foot planted precariously on a hill and the other foot planted firmly in the past. The city's tempestuous history leaps up to surround him on all sides, sometimes engulfing him so completely that he spends his declining years in stubborn contemplation of a past he never knew but which he identifies himself with. This, of course, is an extreme point of view, unfortunately found all too often among powerful people who could contribute to progress if they would stop looking back.

But for San Franciscans generally this gloried, glamorous past adds a peculiar zest to his daily living. It is as though he were born with recollections—of the brawling fortune hunters who came in Forty-nine and left their names, if not their pioneer ways, to families that are now "old" and "respectable." Of the Bonanza Kings, who built their stupefying mansions on Nob Hill and first gave that eminent eminence the reputation for luxury and gaiety that lives on, to a fairly recognizable extent, today. Of the city that perished in the flames of April 18, 1906, and produced the haunting legend (or was it fact?) that there never was a city like the pre-fire San Francisco.

Maybe the late Will Irwin was right when he told me not long before he died, "No, San Francisco isn't what it used to be, but it never was!" But I like to think he was wrong, in a way. I like to think that there is a special magic about San Francisco that can never be burned out, a magic that is created afresh each day out of the never-changing fogs, winds, and hills that surround the eternal Bay.

This love for the past—expressed best by the cable cars and the flower stands and perhaps worst by the hopeless sentimentalists who distrust all change—gives San Francisco a warmth I like.

The removal of a traffic cop from the corner he's occupied for twenty years will bring a flood of protests to the Police Department. If the old Negro doorman outside a department store suddenly turns up absent, the manager will get a dozen phone calls from worried neighbors, asking: "Didn't see Bill out there this morning. Is he sick or something?"

Even town "characters," in the tradition of the legendary Emperor Norton, are laughed with, not at. A stout gentleman named "Tiny" Armstrong, who wears a swallow-tailed coat and a top hat studded with tinfoil stars, walks daily along the midtown streets, leaving in his wake a trail of smiling faces and indulgent comments. He is fed free in many a restaurant, simply because of the attention he attracts. And he is a guest of honor, seated at his own special table, at every meeting of a prominent organization called The Saints and Sinners, which meets in no less a sacroswank spot than the Fairmont.

Then there is the character known only as "Felix," who for years has haunted the stage door of the Golden Gate Theatre. Felix is a tradition, for he'll accept no handout larger than a dime, even in these days of inflation. It all goes back to a black day during the prohibition era, when he accepted a handful of counterfeit fifty-cent pieces from a bootlegger and was forthwith grilled for hours by the police.

Felix immediately decided to limit his demands henceforth to ten cents, figuring that nobody would bother to counterfeit a dime. No dope, he.

A third "institution" who patrols the downtown sidewalks is an ex-vaudevillian (he once appeared with George M. Cohan) named Barney Ferguson, whose special "beat" is the financial district. Immaculate in an ancient velvet-collared black overcoat, complete with fresh carnation, Barney drops in at the various fashionable restaurants each day at noon— where he is likely to give a real estate tip or two to Millionaire Louis Lurie, and a bit of political lowdown to State Senator George Hatfield.

No one, I'm happy to say, has been rude enough to break a tradition of thirty years' standing. His remarks are accepted with deep and thoughtful consideration, and he is often invited to attend meetings of the boards of directors on Montgomery Street. One of Barney's finest moments came at such a meeting, when he was called upon to close the session with a few remarks. Mr. Ferguson merely arose to the top of his five feet three, glanced around at the assembled tycoons, and observed:

"Gentlemen, as I look you over I see that anybody can become a millionaire these days. But how many of you have the talent to become a character?"

In the ensuing expressive silence, Barney made a dignified exit.

The traditions and culture of "the city that knows (period)" have been zealously preserved. There is evidence everywhere. In the country's finest Opera House, a glittering opera season and a self-sustaining symphony orchestra magnificently conducted by Pierre Monteux. In art galleries that draw more visitors annually than New York's. In fine restaurants whose owners seem to realize, instinctively, that theirs is the responsibility of maintaining a world-wide reputation for good food. In art patrons and art lovers who are sharply aware that a "young" city should never turn its back blindly on new ideas and new forms of expression.

And then there's the weather.

True, it's an unpredictable climate—although the weatherman goes right on making his daily predictions in the hope that someday, by pure coincidence, the weather might agree with him. Its very vagaries are what make it attractive. The temperature rarely gets out of its highly publicized 40-low and 80-high slot—and within those forty degrees it's not unusual to encounter a summery sun, a wintry wind, and a film of fog all in forty minutes.

The fog, you say? San Francisco has fewer days of intense fog than Seattle, or even Los Angeles. And when it does come in (not necessarily on little cat feet) it stays only a few hours—long enough to take the curl out of most women's hair, but at the same time toning up their complexion in a way that even Elizabeth Arden might envy.

No, San Franciscans don't object to the fog, unless it happens to come in while they're playing golf or tennis or watching a baseball game. What they do object to is the Hollywood-esque impression that the city is continually submerged under a layer of super-pea soup, through which the foghorns bleat continuously and depressingly while Dashiell Hammett characters slither down alleys, away from the scene of the crime.

San Francisco has fog. And it's remarkably easy to live with.

But, you ask, aren't there any hard, practical reasons why I'm so strong for San Francisco? (The feeling isn't necessarily mutual.)

Lots of them.

As a workingman, I'm proud to be part of the city where labor fought its earliest battles for recognition in the West, and where, as a result, wages are considerably higher and jobs a good deal more secure than elsewhere on the Coast.

As an American, I enjoy the knowledge that minorities from all over the world live here, side by side, in an atmosphere that is truly "cosmopolitan"—that is, remarkably free from condescension, chauvinism, and petty friction. I like the daily sight of Negroes working at self-respecting jobs for the municipal government, running streetcars, handling the grips on a cable car, driving busses. I salute Dr. Herbert Clish, the new superintendent of education, for promptly appointing a Negro as principal of a large school; and I tip my hat to District Attorney Edmund G. "Pat" Brown for appointing the first Negro Assistant District Attorney in San Francisco's history. ("Good politics," you say. In how many cities?) In only a few years, as these things are reckoned, the Chinese and Japanese have become integral parts of the civic scenery—in almost every kind of job and profession in almost every part of the city.

WHY I LIKE SAN FRANCISCO

The San Franciscan is not merely tolerant; that's an offensive word, anyway. It's just that nobody has had to sell him on the idea that people are people—good or bad—regardless of race or color. He knows that from his earliest recollections, for he's gone to school with the great cross section, ridden the cable cars with them, done business with them and their fathers before them.

San Francisco is more than a melting pot. It is many worlds—and one.

But always the continual excitement of living in San Francisco goes back to basic things—like the scenery. The city is good to look at, and there are thousands of windows to see it from. There is something serenely satisfying in the knowledge that the city and its charms are right there to be looked at every day by you, and your neighbor, and the guy on the next hill—all sharing a common love in which there is never jealousy or resentment. That is the warm feeling I get in this cool gray city, the feeling that makes me glad I'm a San Franciscan.

31.

THE GOOD OLD NIGHTS

For reasons that are not always apparent today San Francisco still has a world-wide reputation as a city that comes to life—and what a life!—when the sun goes down.

I don't know. All that must have been part of its flaming youth. But one thing for sure: it must have been quite a town, if you can believe what you still hear from old-timers and can still read in dusty old journals. And the present-day San Franciscan, even if he goes to bed at 8 P.M. and sleeps soundly all night, rather glories in the fable that in his city the thrill-seeker can find all the worst excesses of Port Said, Marseilles, and Shanghai rolled up into one naughty package (delivered in a plain wrapper).

All this is a flock of nonsense now. San Francisco is a lot less "wicked," in the prudish sense of the word, than most of the other large cities in the country. But the legend persists—

a holdover from the hangovers of earlier generations. And, at that, there *is* quite a chunk of evidence that there were some hot nights in the old town.

Let's just say that you can believe what you want to believe about the long nights of yesterday's San Francisco.

You can believe the half-truth of glittering midnight parties in the "Champagne Era," when the bubbly ran in golden torrents and "Little Egypt" danced in the raw atop a table in the Poodle Dog.

You can believe that the Barbary Coast was "a sink of moral pollution," the most depraved section of the most depraved city in America.

You can believe that for one hundred years generations of San Franciscans have done practically nothing but wait uneasily for night to fall, whereupon they leave their tedious offices and homes and wander from one alcoholic adventure to another, consuming fabulous quantities of rich food and fine wine and awakening without a hangover to plan the next evening's pleasures.

Almost without exception the chroniclers of San Francisco's nocturnal past dwell lovingly on the picturesque excesses of "The Paris of America," a fine phrase in its day but a little antiquated today.

"The city that never sleeps!" was another proud cry of the apparently indestructible San Franciscan of old, who could play all night at the Maison Doree and sleep all day—provided, that is, he had a few million dollars drifting in annually from the Big Bonanza.

In fact, the only reproachful note sounded in those days of The Big Nights came from a bitter young man named Frank Norris, who insisted on referring to San Francisco as "The city that never thinks." Not that the objects of Mr. Norris's scorn were too deeply wounded by his opinion. Why think, anyway—except of broiled terrapin at Godey's and a dawn breakfast of broiled steak and quail at Dickey's after a gay night at Bessie Hall's.

Naturally, there is no such thing as a temperate account of San Francisco's night life. History and legend have been blended in a high alcoholic haze until nothing remains but a series of peaks, with a Bacchanalian revel in progress atop each one.

Thus it is that today the San Franciscan looks about at the none-too-exciting night clubs, the very correct and modish hotel supper rooms, and the 1300 conventional bars, and comes to the conclusion that things after dark have slowed down to a yawn. But judging from the record, in about fifty years this same San Franciscan will be reading, with extreme fascination, of the wild splurges of the 1940's, and, appropriately misty-eyed, telling his children a pre-fabricated tale that they will swallow with appropriate gasps.

All this is too bad, really, because from the very beginning the after-dark antics of this Baghdad-by-the-Bay have been a fairly accurate reflection of their era.

A hundred or so years ago the town was topheavy with saloons, with fabulous gambling casinos and all the other appurtenances—of necessity. There was no such thing as a "home life" in this gold-swollen port. "Respectable" citizens were not likely to invite a miner, high-smelling despite his pocketfuls of gold dust, into their homes for a quiet dinner and an evening with the stereopticons.

No, there was only one place to go at night in the early Fifties—and that was "out," on the town. Undoubtedly to the El Dorado, the first saloon and gambling house, where "America's greatest bartender," Professor Jerry Thomas, served his immortal inventions, the Blue Blazer and the Tom and Jerry. Or perhaps to the Bella Union, where one of the croupiers was a beautiful Frenchwoman named Mme. Simone Jules, and there was a singer-violinist named Charley Schultze, described by Herbert Asbury as the first man in San Francisco, "and probably in the United States," to sing the famous song, "Aloha."

And I suppose it's rather typical of the times that the first piece of fiction written and printed in California was a tract entitled "Punch Drinking and Its Effects," published in 1847.

The "café society" of the middle Fifties was just as hard as the gold on which it was founded. There was nothing to do after dark but drink or gamble, both to excess. "Legitimate" shows consisted mainly of traveling circuses or third-rate plays. Women were such a rarity that saloonfuls of men would rush to the doors and gape after a lookout's shout: "Hey! A woman is passing by!"

And as late as 1869, according to one lovely legend, an infant, held in its mother's arms at a theater, began to cry—whereupon a man in the pit leaped to his feet and shouted:

225

"Stop those fiddles, and let the baby cry. I haven't heard such a sound in ten years!" The audience applauded, the orchestra stopped, and the baby continued its performance for the appreciative gathering.

But as the years rolled by and San Francisco grew, the pattern of night life split. For the thrill-seekers and the depraved, the Barbary Coast sprang up on Pacific (or "Terrific") Street. For the rich young men of the Bonanza spoils there were the delights of the Palace and the famed French restaurants. History records no middle ground. Those who played beside the Bay at night were either dandies toying with a "Black Velvet" at the Reception Saloon at Kearny and Sutter, or lost souls frolicking lewdly on the Barbary Coast, "the wickedest spot on earth."

And yet Clarence E. Edwords, who visited the coast many times at the height of its ill fame, reports that he saw "nothing shocking to our moral sense that equaled what I have seen in New York, or in some of the most fashionable hotels and restaurants of San Francisco on New Year's Eve." For along with open vice, the Coast produced dance crazes that swept the country. The Texas Tommy, the Grizzly Bear— these were first performed in the dance halls of the Barbary Coast.

Insists Edwords: "There was light and life and laughter that drew crowds nightly." But, apparently, that's not the Barbary Coast that San Francisco wants to remember.

At any rate, San Francisco in the Nineties was a fluid city. There was one saloon for every ninety-five inhabitants. "The

Cocktail Route" was an institution, and every day at 5 P.M., our leading citizens consulted their big gold watches, left their offices, and sauntered along Market, up Kearny to Sutter and over to Powell, eating a Lucullan fill of free lunches and drinking twenty or thirty champagne cocktails, all without losing their appetites or staggering even slightly.

What were the poor people doing? I don't know, for the records of the "Champagne Age" in San Francisco are devoted exclusively to the after-dark recreations of such dandies as Jimmy Phelan and Will Tevis, Walter Hobart and Charlie Fair, Lucky Baldwin, Ned Greenway, and Ward McAllister, Jr.

The only note of normalcy is provided by a clipping from the Oakland *Daily Transcript,* which noted: "The police of San Francisco arrested 488 drunks last month, only eight of which were 'common' ones. Drunks in that town are generally of a remarkable character."

Nothing sobered San Francisco more devastatingly than the 1906 fire-quake. The Barbary Coast dives were reduced to smoking ruins, and although they were rebuilt rapidly and flourished again, they were attacked incessantly by the righteous, and the inevitable was near. Famous saloons and restaurants disappeared, and with it their old flavor. Gone forever was the old Palace. Overnight, San Francisco aged to the point of maturity.

There were still cafés and French restaurants with naughty "rooms upstairs," but night life took on a new dignity. San Francisco had grown up to the problems of a big city, and the pursuit of pleasure became secondary. And with the advent of Prohibition, night life here became more or less what night life was like in every city in the country—a fugitive thing of rotgut liquor, bootleggers, sporadic raids, and the flask on the hip.

Not that there wasn't plenty to do. There was dignified dancing at the dignified Fairmont, to an orchestra containing a violinist named Paul Whiteman. Art Hickman was playing "jazz" in the Rose Room of the St. Francis. And Tait's Pavo Real was highly favored and flavored, with a couple of kids named Fanchon and Marco producing the shows. An ex-bus boy named Rudolf Valentino danced, not too badly.

Out of all this evolves the San Francisco of today—a responsible city, rather set in its ways. And, as in the past, the night life measures the tempo of the times.

This era could never produce a city-shaking episode like "Little Egypt" dancing in the nude atop a table in the Poodle Dog. The inventor of a new drink would hardly be extolled as "that great benefactor of mankind" as Duncan Nichol was for concocting the Pisco Punch. It isn't likely that a fat girl performing a writhing sensual dance would be a sensation for long—like Gyp was with her "Dance of the Seven Veils" at Red Kelly's Midway on the old Coast. Today, she'd be arrested immediately, and Red along with her.

These nights, San Francisco is no longer "the city that never sleeps," except for the rounders who know the few spots that "cheat." Any gay abandon reminiscent of the flavorful past can be found only in a couple of dives along Mason

Street, or in a few unself-conscious places in the Post-Fill-more "Little Harlem" district.

Certainly visitors still marvel at the capacity of San Franciscans to drink, with hardly visible effect, from the cocktail hour till 2 A.M. or later. The tinkle of ice in tall glasses can still be heard loudly every night, from the numerous bars of the Fairmont to the saloons of Skid Road. Perhaps the best explanation for this well-slaked thirst was given back in 1853 by a visiting woman newspaper correspondent, who enthused:

"Hail to the San Franciscan—whose cool climate both fosters a desire for liquor and enables him to carry it!"

32.

THE OTHER SIDE OF THE TRACKS

San Francisco is not all white towers and rolling hills and filmy fog. There is more to be seen than the smart shops, the big hotels, and the surface "color" that first strike the tourist's eye and fancy. Unfortunately, such miracles as Golden Gate Park and the Golden Gate Bridge tell only a small, if eminently pleasant, part of the San Francisco story.

The Chamber of Commerce, which seems never to have heard about six people living in one tiny room in the Fillmore district and which would rather not talk about the tuberculosis rate in Chinatown, would also be just as happy if you didn't hear about San Francisco's Skid Road, where the down-and-outers mingle with the has-beens and the never-wassers in an atmosphere of failure and cheap wine and greasy food.

Every big city has its Skid Road, the home of the homeless, where pockets and hearts are always empty and pawnshop windows are always full. In some cities the district is tucked away, out of sight, where the "respectable" citizen doesn't have to look at it every day and perhaps feel slight pangs of conscience.

But San Francisco's Skid Road can't be ignored so easily. It dirties the fringes of the city's teeming center. It spreads like a dark cancer along Third Street and Fourth, leaving its smudges on Mission and Howard and Folsom. It is a daily irony of failure rubbing elbows with success, a hard fact of life that San Francisco has to live with day and night.

The well-to-do commuters, on their way to the Third and Townsend station to catch the trains that take them to their Peninsula homes, pass daily through the heart of Skid Road. The well-to-do merchants whose offices are still in this old neighborhood, roll through its alleys in their limousines, their chauffeurs keeping a sharp watch for lurching drunks and the canned-heat bums. You can sometimes smell the unmistakable aura of Skid Road—the sherry wine, the sodden hamburger, the disinfectant, the poverty—as you step into the Palace Hotel for a drink in one of its fashionable bars.

This is Skid Road, where the men who might as well be dead go on living, perhaps gathering the needed ounce of strength from their realization that there are so many others as miserable as they. In their patched, castoff clothing and their rotting shoes, they stand in knots on the corners, talking of better days, of their last meal, of their next drink.

Meanwhile, the big cars purr by, their occupants studiously avoiding even a glance at the miserable ones who stand like living indictments of The System. The tourists pass through in big sightseeing busses, feeling the smug, delicious thrill of "slumming" comfortably, hermetically sealed from the squalor of a few feet away. The cops patrol the streets, in pairs, for here in Skid Road they are surrounded by criminals—it being a crime to be a failure in The Land of Opportunity.

Certainly there is color along Skid Road—color, and a certain hard character, and certainly hard characters. There are fine old-time saloons stocking the best liquors and serving good food. There are decent little hotels where four bits will get you a reasonably comfortable bed. There are interesting old guys who have saved a little money and could move elsewhere, but who prefer to live out their days among the card-rooms and bookie joints and pubs where they can sit and talk with their own kind.

The "Mark Hopkins" of the Road is Breen's, a first-class saloon on Third Street, down the alley from the back end of the Palace. In Breen's you'll find the classic montage of bums and businessmen, sightseers and habitués, newspapermen and socialites, mingling in an atmosphere that combines just enough earthiness with just enough respectability.

It was the one-hundred-proof fascination of Breen's that not so long ago unseated a mighty named Charles Stanley Sackett, somewhat of a legend in the hotel business. The elegant Charles Stanley, who once managed the Vanderbilt Hotel in New York and buddied around with the likes of

Luscious Lucius Beebe, is the walrus-mustached prototype of Peter Arno's harried cartoon character. As a hotel man, he was the very model of a modern major-domo.

Eventually, Sackett charmed himself into the not inconsiderable job of manager of the Palace Hotel, over which he presided in spats, striped trousers, morning coat, and pearl-studded ascot. But despite the fact that he exuded no end of Continental dignity and expensive cologne, he soon got wind of the bonded bourbons and unbonded prices of Breen's —which, as we have stated, is located at the corner of an alley in the regal shadow of the Palace.

The byways of Skid Road soon had a new legend—the legend of the bespatted, beboutonniered, mustached boniface of the Palace trotting down the alley to Breen's for his mid-afternoon pick-me-up and even a late evening knock-me-down. It was inevitable that Charles Stanley and the Palace were not long for each other. The Palace is right where it has always been. Sackett retreated, without losing a dram of his dignity, to the stewardship of a small upcountry hotel, which, he once said wistfully, "is roughly the size of the Vanderbilt in New York. The Vanderbilt lobby, that is."

But Charles Stanley Sackett's tale is one of the more unusual facets of life along San Francisco's Skid Road.

More closely fitting the accepted pattern, I suppose, was the recent death of a once-prominent attorney, who was found, surrounded by empty bottles of cheap liquor, in a dirty flop-house bed. His erstwhile confreres in the legal fraternity, occupying suites of offices only three blocks away on the "right" side of Market, were of course shocked by the discovery. "If he had only told us he needed help," they all said in spurious tones of shocked surprise—for they had all seen him many times and had bothered only to look the other way.

Then there is the white-haired, wise-eyed canned-heat bum who is called "Professor," because he was, once, before he learned to like the bottle more than he liked teaching. And "Doc," who now and then looks at his trembling hands and wonders how he was ever able to perform an operation. And the ex-speculator, referred to derisively as "J. P.," who plucks newspapers out of trash cans so he can peruse the stock-market quotations, as he used to do in his nearby Montgomery Street office—a man who is down and out because he thought the market would keep going onward and upward.

These are some of the noted characters who shuffle slowly along dirty sidewalks dotted with empty wine bottles, their eyes filled with an equal emptiness, their ears deaf to the blare of the Salvation Army band and the monotonous mumble of "Razors, a nickel. A good overcoat, five bucks. Dime for a toothbrush" from the thieves who peddle their stolen wares along the curbs.

There is always news, of a peculiar quality, along Third Street and Howard and Mission.

I remember the day the late Mayor Angelo Rossi picked up a destitute couple and their four children near Third and Mission. They looked so miserable and lost, standing there hand in hand, that he ordered his limousine to stop. Then he took them to the City Hall, where he fed and clothed them and gave them transportation to another city, where they had relatives.

But while they were at the Hall, Angelo noticed suddenly that the wife was wearing brand-new shoes. The husband answered his question:

"My wife was barefoot when we got to San Francisco. We were standing outside a shoe store, lookin' in the winder, and a strange man walked up, dug in his pocket, and gave her three bucks for a pair. He said he lived in some hotel near by, and used to be a famous prize fighter. He said his name was Tom Sharkey."

It was "Sailor Tom" Sharkey, immortal of ring history, conqueror of Fitzsimmons in eight rounds, now old, grizzled, and retired to a little room in a small hotel just around the corner from nowhere in the heart of Skid Road.

An even stranger drama has been enacted daily for more than a year in a saloon on Howard Street. While hangers-on watch with expressions that are almost tender, a kid named Johnny, a veteran of World War II, moves slowly and carefully over to an ancient panhandler called Monty, and slips him a dime, and sometimes a quarter.

"Thanks, thanksalot, Johnny," says Monty, with a smile. "Okay, f'get it," grunts Johnny, moving away again.

Johnny, the kid, has never let on to Monty that he's blind. Monty? He's blind too.

The funny, and yet unfunny, antics of Skid Road's panhandlers are an endless source of material for columnists and cocktail conversationalists. Some of the stories are fables, and most of them have a tendency to fall flat, if only because there is no basic humor in the plight of a human being reduced to the point of begging. However, here are a few that are true, with perhaps a surface smile mixed in to justify them.

I happened to be in Superior Judge Albert Wollenberg's court one day when a sad-eyed Skid Rowgue went on trial on two counts of robbery. According to the testimony, he had held up a man on Third Street and relieved him of fifty-five cents, after which he had dashed around a corner, stuck up another gent, and robbed him of a dollar.

"Now," questioned Deputy District Attorney Elton Lawless, "why did you commit these crimes?"

The question irritated Deputy Public Defender Abe Dresow. "Because, Mr. Lawless," he snapped, "he happened to be hungry, that's why."

"If that's the case," shot back Lawless, "why didn't he go eat after he'd robbed the first victim?"

The Skid Rowgue, drowsing on the stand, suddenly came to life. Looking up at Judge Wollenberg, he demanded testily: "Where in this town kinya get anything decent to eat for fifty-five cents?"

Even more celebrated is the equally true story of a gay and giddy stew who waddled out of a Third Street bar, flopped down behind the wheel of a parked, unguarded Yellow Cab, and drove it four frightening blocks before he was captured.

THE OTHER SIDE OF THE TRACKS

He came up for trial before Superior Judge Alden Ames on a slight charge of grand theft, and was defended by Deputy Public Defender Billy McDonnell. McDonnell's first question to the defendant was "Why did you take this cab?"

The now quite sober Skidkid silently fished around in his pockets, withdrew a dirty, torn card, and presented it to McDonnell. The card, part of an old Yellow Cab advertisement, read: "When you have been drinking, take a cab!"

It was about a year ago that the Bank of America launched a "Let's Get Better Acquainted!" advertising campaign, slanted at breaking down the psychological barriers between the newcomers to California and the old-timers. A few days later, into the Powell and Market branch walked a fugitive from Third and Howard, who draped himself in front of a teller's window and beamed: "Hiya. I been reading your ads and I thought I'd drop in. I wanna get acquainted with some money!"

Warren Shannon, a one-time city supervisor, and his late great friend, Publisher A. R. O'Brien, were in the habit of strolling the streets of Skid Road, merely to pass out a few dollars and exchange a little conversation with the panhandlers. They were stopped one night by a moocher who related tearfully that he was sick, hungry, and broke, and only wanted money for a bed.

"O.K.," said O'Brien, dredging up a bill. "Here's a dollar. Give me fifty cents' change."

The "broke" one promptly handed over a half-dollar,

whereupon O'Brien laughed. "Aha! I knew you were lying—but here's the money anyhow."

"But," answered the surprised beggar, pocketing the buck, "if you knew I was lyin', why do I get the dough?"

"For telling the truth," smiled O'Brien as he walked away.

Wilson Mizner, the late humorist who spent many years around San Francisco, had a favorite fable about a pair of Nob Hill grande dames who went "slumming" one night along Third Street. In the first block they were stopped by a wise old hand who sensed an easy mark.

"Y'gotta help me, ladies," he croaked. "I ain't had nothin' to eat for three days."

The first member of Nobhillity was shocked. She turned to her companion. "Did you hear that?" she asked with a tear in her voice. "This man says he hasn't eaten for three days."

Then she turned back to the hopeful panhandler, laid a hand on his shoulder, and said firmly: "My good man, you must *force* yourself to eat!"

This, then, is Skid Road, where the misfits fit together in a half-world of the half-dead, a stone's throw (the stone is thrown at them) from all that spells success and respectability. Skid Road, where the booze is cheap and searing, where a man can raise a thirst but not always the money to slake it, where human dignity is peddled on any corner for a thin dime. Almost everything is thin down here in the hard heart of the city, but only the thick-skinned survive.

Even the cops have a special approach, a special kind of

cruel humor along Skid Road. At Third and Howard, where the down-and-outers lounge and slump all day and night against lampposts and fire hydrants and walls, a cop one day walked out into the middle of the intersection and yelled at the mob:

"Awright, you guys, let's straighten up around here. Ya wanna give this corner a bad name?"

He got his laugh—a cackling, empty, hideous kind of laugh that reverberated and filtered down the alleys and was lost, even as those who could still laugh at themselves are lost.

33.

SOUNDS IN THE NIGHT

The voices of San Francisco are many. The ceaseless click-clacking of the cables in their slots, the chuckling of California Street's red bricks under your automobile tires, the sloshy groaning of the pilings along the Embarcadero, the unique thwack of the old "bird-cage" traffic signals—these are sounds peculiar to the city.

But dominating them all are the intermittent, seemingly disordered voices of the foghorns on a shrouded night, calling to each other across the Bay in fits and starts that have kept thousands of San Franciscans awake for thousands of nights.

A hopeless insomniac, it took me months of watchful waiting in a rumpled bed even to figure out how many foghorns are ranged around the harbor. It took even longer to decide which one is which. But now, I'm happy to say, I can relax with my sleeping tablets. The mystery is solved. It took a few years off my life, but then, who can afford to live these days?

There are six dominant foghorns in the Bay, and I've got the Coast Guard to confirm me. And all six have distinguishing characteristics. With this dearly-bought information, plus a few sleepless nights, you should be able to decipher them too.

First, the Point Bonita horn. That blasts for one second, is silent two seconds, then blasts for two seconds and is silent for twenty-five seconds. A rugged diaphone, that. Took me all one night with a stop watch to figure it out.

You're also kept awake by the horn at Mile Rock. That's comparatively simple, once you've distinguished it. The Mile Rock Martha Raye yells for three seconds and is silent for twenty-seven seconds, and so on, over and over.

The foghorn at Point Diablo is another honey in the night. Of course, being a siren, it can be detected in a hurry, but figuring out its characteristics is another thing. It all adds up to this: Blast four seconds, silent two seconds, blast four seconds, silent twenty seconds, et cetera. Don't ask why; that's the way it is.

The Golden Gate Bridge's foghorn is a "chime diaphragm," if you follow me, and it blasts for one second, is silent for two seconds, gives out again for a second, and is then silent for thirty seconds. The horn at Lime Point sounds two seconds, lays off for two seconds, comes on again for four seconds, and relaxes for twenty-two seconds. The sixth and final big foghorn is the one on Alcatraz—on two seconds, off two, on two, and silent for twenty-four.

A meaningless jumble of sounds in the night? Seems that way at first, but when you put them all together, decipher the various distinguishing sounds, and match the blast periods with the silences, you see that they add up to a definite pattern designed *not* to keep you awake all night but to help the mariner who's groping his way through the soup into the harbor.

Besides, the foghorn situation is much better than it used to be.

Back in 1937, when the Golden Gate Bridge was first opened, the foghorn on the span was so loud that it rattled windows all over the Sea Cliff sector. The sleepless residents finally screamed so poignantly that the strength of the horn was greatly reduced, and these nights you're hearing just an anemic version of what the Gate bridge's horn could do if it really tried. Be thankful.

Furthermore, it was less than one hundred years ago that foghorns in this area consisted of cannon blasting in the night. The first fog warning was a 24-pounder transferred from Benecia Arsenal to Bonita Point Light Station. In charge of the affair was a Sergeant Maloney, whose instructions, dated August 5, 1855, went like this:

"You are charged with the firing of the 24-pounder gun placed at Point Bonita as a fog signal, and will proceed thither tomorrow with the powder purchased for same. Your directions are to fire the gun every half-hour during fogs at the

entrance to the Bay, whether they occur at night or in the day
—the firing being made at the hours and half-hours of San
Francisco mean time."

And Sergeant Maloney, whoever he was, had a mean time.
Two months after taking over the job (to escape K.P., no
doubt) he described sadly in his diary:

"I cannot find any person here to relieve me not five minutes. I have been up three days and nights and had only two
hours' rest, and am nearly used up. All the rest I would re-
quire in the twenty-four hours is two, if I could only get it."

Poor Maloney. Despite his lament, he was stuck with the
thankless job till 1857, when his foghorn cannon was discon-
tinued as too expensive and no good anyway. The sergeant
burned up $2000 worth of gunpowder a year, and half the
ships entering the Bay couldn't hear his cannon. He was relieved, and later no doubt became a brigadier general in
the Services of Supply.

34.

STRANGER IN THE SUNSET

The Sunset District—or "Doelger Row"—has been the victim of more snide remarks in the past few years than any other section of town.

In a way, of course, that's only natural. There's something vaguely amusing about those blocks of wedding-cake houses, floating on sand and FHA loans, all looking alike, smelling alike, and costing alike.

The gags about the Sunset are all alike too. You can't drive a nail in your wall to hang a picture without checking with the guy next door—to make sure *he* has a picture to hang on the other end. In the morning, when your wife asks you: "How do you want your eggs, dear?" a husband seven houses down answers, "Scrambled." And so on.

But don't get the idea that the Sunset is mom'n'populated with prosaic young middle-class couples all equipped with one (1) child, one (1) car, and all having a hard time meeting those easy monthly payments. Over their blended whisky old-fashioneds (with built-in cherries) the Sunsettlers have something exciting to talk about. In fact, something to shake the district down to its very foundations, if it had any.

A Stranger has moved into their midst. He lives in a house that looks just like the house to the left, the right, and across the way. But the Stranger is different. He lives alone—most of the time. He comes and goes at strange hours in the middle of the night. His neighbors peek at him suspiciously through their Venetian blinds. He's the Number-1 topic of conversation in every cubicle built for two.

For the Stranger is a mobster.

He looks as out of place in the Sunset as a Frank Lloyd Wright house. "Butch"—the handle hung on him by the Doelger Rowgues—is big and burly, and he wears clothes that cling to him like they really cared. His car is black, with a long, shiny nose that sneers at people.

His neighbors on —th Avenue know a lot about Butch. In fact, some of them used to stage "Let's watch Butch" parties in various homes near his, instead of going to the movies. At times they were much more entertaining too.

There was the night, for instance, he threw one of his girl friends out of his house. He threw her out the way a mobster is supposed to—even one who lives in the Sunset. First, she came hurtling down the stairs and landed right on her ear, which she proceeded to massage tenderly. Then, in quick succession, out flew her coat, bag, and overnight case. She limped off in the direction of Lincoln Way, and for blocks around the phones jangled the news.

Then there was the thrilling night five hoods showed up in their own black sedan. One of them got out and yelled "Hey, Butch! Open up!" No answer. Four of the schmos got out while the fifth remained behind the wheel, with the motor idling. The four gents cased the jernt, found everything locked, and proceeded to take one of the doors off its hinges with a screwdriver. A few minutes later they reappeared on peaceful —th Avenue, climbed back into the car, and roared away.

A couple of days later Butch came back to his little house that looks just like the house to the left, to the right, and across the way. His car was thick with dust. When his sharp eye noticed the job on his door he called the cops and raised a fuss. Isn't a peace-loving citizen of the Sunset entitled to some protection?

Butch probably realizes that he's a little out of place in his surroundings. The neighbors recall one slightly poignant attempt he made to become a member of the stuccommunity he lives in. One sunny Sunday morning he walked out of his slice of wedding cake, stood on the sidewalk for a minute, and noticed a young wife watering the lawn across the street.

"Good morning!" he called.

She dropped the hose and ran inside.

On another occasion some of the young married settlers were having a cocktail party a couple of doors down from

Butch's. "Hey," suggested a gent who'd had one too many ready-mixed martinis. "Le's invite Butch, huh? Mebbe we can find out what he's up to. Joe, go over and ask him." Joe said, "Pete, you ask him." Pete passed the buck to Ed. They finally drew straws and Joe got the short end. He came back in a few minutes empty-handed.

"I guess I got no guts," he sighed. "I got all the way up to his door and I just couldn't ring the bell. Gimme a drink."

The prize incident on —th Avenue took place one morning when Butch, looking strangely out of place in slacks and sport shirt, was struggling with a flat tire on his car. Slowly, one by one, the neighbors' kids, who'd heard their parents discussing the mobster, gathered around silently to watch him at work.

But one moppet, a little more daring than the others, began to taunt him. "You really a gangster?" he asked. Butch grunted. "How many guys you killed, mister?" persisted the tyke. "Get lost, kid," suggested Butch. When the tire-changing job was finally finished, the tots all scattered—except the fresh one. He watched Butch disappear into the garage, then he walked up to the door and banged on it. "Open up!" he hooted. "I'm Dick Tracy!"

Slowly the garage door opened a trifle. While a group of neighbors across the way stared in frozen fright a big black automatic stuck its nose around the corner of the door. Rooted, the kid looked bug-eyed into the muzzle. Butch's finger squeezed the trigger.

The kid was hit squarely between the eyes—with a stream of water.

Things are a trifle dull these nights on —th Avenue in the heart of the Sunset district. Butch's house still looks like all the houses on the block, except the Venetian blinds are closed tight and the windows are dirty.

They came for Butch one recent day, and there was a lot of talk about bookies and smuggling. "A year," said the judge.

Butch is pretty unhappy in jail. "It's the monotony that gets me," he says, looking balefully around his cell, which is just like the one to the left, to the right, and across the way.

35.

A ROOM WITH A VIEW

The common denominator of housing in San Francisco is a view.

With the sweeping expanse of hills, harbor, and Bay stretching for miles outside his window, the man in his tiny $50-a-month wooden shack on Telegraph Hill is as rich—scenically—as the millionaire in his lavish apartment next door. And he is infinitely richer than the well-off burgher in his St. Francis Wood mansion, whose windows can't even see around the next corner.

The San Franciscan never tires of looking at the face of his city. Thousands of them prefer to walk to work every morning, so they can gaze anew at the sights that never seem to be quite the same two days in a row. There is always a stray strand of fog across the sun to cast a new light over the rambling hills, there is always the Pacific tang to put a new bounce into your steps, there seems always to be the little inviting byway that somehow you failed to notice yesterday.

But especially at home the San Franciscan wants to keep gazing over the city he never sees enough of. If he has a few extra dollars to spend, he is likely to invest them in a larger front-room window, or in a deck he can step onto with a tourist and say, with the smug assurance of one who is about to unfold certified wonders,

"Look! Where can you see anything like *that!*"

I, for instance, live in a little three-room apartment on the "poor man's" side of Nob Hill. It isn't the most convenient place in town. The wayward elevator's motions are almost as horizontal as they are vertical, and every time it starts, the whole building shakes. My rooms are as small as large closets—and there aren't any closets.

It has only one thing—a huge, plate-glass living room window, and that's enough.

For from my window I can see San Francisco framed and preserved under glass.

On a clear day I can look off to the left and see Alcatraz floating motionless behind a pane, and far around to the right, the valley of the financial district, where the tall buildings grow. Before me stretches the flatness of Chinatown—chow-meingling around the edges with North Beach—and I can reflect comfortably that the people from lands a world apart are neighbors here, and good ones. I can look out toward the ageless Bay and tell what time it is, for the Ferry Building is my grandfather's clock—and late at night, when the darkness has drawn a shade over my window, I can hear the ship's bell down at the water front clanging out 4 A.M.

I can see a world of transportation from my window, for the Bridge is arranged neatly across the middle of it, like a million-dollar ornament built expressly to be admired by my guests. And beneath the Bridge the last two ferryboats shuttle endlessly back and forth on invisible tracks, looking as lonely as they must feel, now that so many of their counterparts have vanished. Across their white wake cut the black freighters, going slowly and sullenly about their business. And between them all dance the bright sails of the tiny yachts, lighter than fluff on the swelling breast of the Bay.

I can see history from my window, for when the sun cocks a red eyebrow over the rim of the Oakland hills at 5 A.M. there is a silence of the ages over the whole magnificent scene —and in the dim, magical light the metropolis loses its identity, and it might as well be the dawn of a new day in 1648, barren and majestic. Telegraph Hill is just a blob to the left, and for all you know Coit Tower is once again the semaphore signaling ships into the Bay. There are still shadows at play in the canyon of California Street, where Ralston and Sharon wrestled for an empire—and it could be 1929 in the lighted office high atop the Russ Building, and inside sits a broken broker, looking from his ledger to the window and back again. And that dark figure shuffling through Waverly Place must be Fung Jing Toy—"Little Pete"—or one of his hatchet men, at the very least.

I can see people from my window. The accordion and

salami makers of Columbus Avenue, busily manufacturing music for the ears and dissonance for the breath. The youngest generation of Chinatown, playing baseball in the alleys, where the smell of opium once hovered like a rotting flower. The impatient passengers, tumbling out of their seats to help the aged Sacramento Street bus climb Nob Hill. And the oldsters of North Beach, sitting out the twilight of their lives in the sunlight of Washington Square.

I can see the fog from my window, venturing in like the unwelcome guest it must know it is by this time. So first, with an apologetic shrug, it wraps its mantle around Alcatraz, as though to say: "Well, you won't miss seeing *this*, anyway." But soon it is drawn irresistibly to the whiteness of Coit Tower, first toying daintily with it, then suddenly gobbling it whole before your very eyes. Nurtured by this solid meal, the fog lunges at the Appraisers' Building, obliterating its mass with obvious relish, and then slides happily into the Bay, slithering venomously onto the Bridge and gobbling its succulent orange lights one by one. Then, fatter than a well-fed python, our monster from the sea settles down to sleep, and the city must sleep with it.

I can see odds and ends of a civilization from my window. Sun bathers, stretched out on the flatness of an apartment-house roof, every line in every body straining toward the thin, wind-cut sun. Flower boxes on window sills, always the most poignant gesture of the city dweller who yearns for a piece of land. The haze of lights from the produce district, the cupboard for Old Mother San Francisco. The shabby

252

grayness of the Hall of Justice, looking no more imposing than the dregs who plead for humanity there. The forest of bare flagpoles atop a dozen office buildings, waiting for the holiday—or the death—that will make them blossom into color. The tiny one-man shops of Kearny Street—the bottom rungs of a financial structure that gets bigger and bulkier as it climbs toward the top. (And it reaches the top just one block away, its foundations resting on filled-in land.)

I can see lights from my window. The shimmering sparkle of the East Bay, spread over the hills like a million fireflies —ah, how distance lends enchantment. The red neon glow from the North Beach hamburger belt, reflecting up against the rear end of Telegraph Hill. The Alcatraz beacon, silhouetting the graceful spires of Sts. Peter and Paul for an instant on each round. The gold-drenched Shell Building, a monument to oil that is holy. The phony external finery of the saloons along Columbus Avenue and Broadway, making the night spot a bright spot in their own little gayliwick.

These are the things I can see from my window—sitting in one world and looking out on another. The heart of a city— sous-glace—silent as a pretalking picture, yet making glad and sad noises for my eyes. Ever-changing, never-changing San Francisco!

36.

MR. SAN FRANCISCO

Every "Mr. San Francisco," no matter what his age, has one thing in common. He begins developing sharp memories about his city at a surprisingly early age, and the longer he lives with them, the more important and the more significant they come—until finally, as he nears the end of the road, they play a dominant role in his life.

In a way, this is one of the most revealing things to know about San Francisco. For this continual backward-thinking and backward-looking, living strongly among some of the city's leaders, explains a lot of "mysteries." It helps explain antiquated "gingerbread" housing, cable cars that are as much a problem as they are picturesque, and ancient monuments stuck smack in the middle of the traffic stream.

On the other hand, of course, it also explains old restaurants with colorful old waiters who know every customer by his first name. It explains a kind of gracious, if mauve, mode of living in mansions that should have been torn down long ago. It explains hundreds of major businesses handed down from father to son and still run "family" style—and a distinctive kind of open-hearted friendliness and frankness among the older settlers.

Just for fun, let's look at some of these slightly strange, slightly wonderful people we call "Mr. San Francisco."

If he's in his seventies, he's telling stories now of what he said to Lucky Baldwin and how Bill Ralston used to come to him for financial advice—and, what's more, by this time he's believing them himself . . . Of course he was excited when his grandson came sailing back from overseas at the end of World War II—because he'd done exactly the same thing a few years earlier; only his admiral was named Dewey . . . Every time he goes to a restaurant, he gets furious about the three dollar steaks and recalls the ones he used to devour for fifty cents, with everything; but he forgets that fifty cents is what some people used to work all day to earn too . . . And the only way you can stop him from ranting about the hopelessly low morals of the present generation is to start him reminiscing about his conquests in the private dining rooms at Blanco's.

But right now his principal complaint is that while he was born here and hopes to die here, he can't be buried in San Francisco because all the cemeteries are in San Mateo; so, being the stubborn pioneer type, he'll probably go right on living.

If he's in his fifties, the only reason he's alive today, he'll want you to know eventually, is that he tripped and fell early on the morning of April 18, 1906, and thereby escaped being buried under a toppling chimney—but only by a matter of inches, mind you . . . As a kid, his idea of sport was crossing the reins of the Chinese laundryman's horse, hurling cobbles down the Webster Street hill and listening till they konked resoundingly off the end of the Union Street trolley; and maybe, on a particularly daring occasion, sneaking up behind a Chinese on a cable car and tying his queue to a post (or trying to) . . . He faintly remembers staring bug-eyed at Cannon the Fat Man, all 780 pounds of him, at the old Chutes, and his happiest moments came on Saturdays, when his father would take him to lunch, at Herbert's Bachelor Restaurant (men only) and then to the Orpheum— where, he's quite sure, he saw everybody who ever amounted to anything in show business, and all on the same bill . . . He still goes to dinner once a week at "Shorty" Roberts' place out at the Beach, because it reminds him of the first time he took his girl there in the family Winton . . . And once in a while he stands all alone for a few minutes in the drab Ferry Building, recalling those wonderful Sunday mornings when they all used to meet "under the Ferry clock" and sail across the Bay for a hike to Alpine Dam or Muir Woods; he can still see the bright sweaters, still feel the weight of the knapsack, still hear the singing and the harmonicas and the rhythmic splash of the paddles.

But he's too young a man to live on memories alone; right now he's looking forward to Sunday—when he'll drive with his wife through Golden Gate Park and eventually break the silence by murmuring: "Say, darling, remember when we——? . . ."

If he's in his forties, he used to go to Amelio's when it was a celebrated speakeasy, and many's the night he whiled away in the Towne Club and got disgustingly torchy while Bobbe Gram sang something pretty racy called "I'm Drunk with Love," and why the stuff he drank didn't kill him, he'll never know, although he suspects that some day his liver will be studied with deep interest by medical students . . . As far as entertainment goes, he knows dambwell there'll never be anything to compare with Walt Roesner's symphony orchestra and the Fanchon-Marco revues in the early days of the Fox Theatre . . . He hasn't been to a baseball game since Bert Ellison managed the Seals, and he follows the football season with nothing more than tolerance, for wasn't he on the side lines when Biff Hoffman and Ernie Nevers pounded to glory for Stanford? Of course—who wasn't? . . . The only reason he doesn't get too impatient while driving his car inch by inch across the gosh-jammed Bay Bridge is that he's busy telling you how he once waited three hours for an auto ferry from Oakland. And as for night life—well, he hasn't been to the Mark Hopkins since Anson

Weeks was there, and he had a date every night with Anson's deep-voiced singer, June MacCloy; of course—who didn't.

All in all, a very nice guy, not too successful, not too ambitious, and slightly cynical about the whole thing. Maybe because he still remembers the proudest day of his business career, when he had enough money in the bank to go out to Van Ness Avenue and buy that Chrysler "77" roadster he'd always wanted. Gleaming with pride, he parked it in front of his office on Montgomery Street and rushed inside to spread the good news. But when he came back out, his car was crushed in the middle—under the body of a broker who had leaped out of the top-floor window. A sunny day in October. The year: 1929.

If he's in his twenties he finds himself thinking more and more about the sunny world he knew before December 1941, and sometimes, in a dark splash of bitterness, he tells you that he has already lived his life, and there's nothing ahead for his generation but question marks and towering clouds shaped like mushrooms . . . He has fought his war and he doesn't want to fight another one—he wants to go back to the few good years he knew. If he had to pick a symbol of what he means, he'd point to Treasure Island, now flat, drab, and ugly; he remembers it as a place of lightness and brightness, filled with magic fountains and far-off music and flowers that smelled like perfume ads read . . . Meanwhile, you see him and his kind flitting restlessly around San Francisco, from one end to the other, drinking a little too much, talking a kind of jumbled-up patois shaped by the Army and shabby sophistication, and all the time looking—for a girl, for a quick way to make a buck, for something, anything that will scatter the doubts that fill his mind.

Not that he's the unhappiest guy in the world; nobody can be completely unhappy—in San Francisco.

If he was born yesterday he might turn out to be the luckiest Mr. San Francisco of them all.

Maybe by the time he's old enough to have his own door key there'll be enough houses for everybody, and the Great Housing Shortage of Forty-nine will merely be something for the old-timers to cackle over.

Maybe by the time he's old enough to go where he wants to go by himself there'll be endless streams of silent streetcars and air-conditioned, fumeless busses.

Maybe by the time he's old enough to chew on a steak he'll be able to afford one, and maybe the only thing he'll know about war is that it's something his father tries to talk about when he's in a reminiscing mood (and nobody else will listen).

And maybe, if he's *real* lucky, there won't even be such a word as "maybe"—for this "Mr. San Francisco" of tomorrow.

37.

BAGHDAD-BY-THE-BAY (REPRISE)

The warm magic of a spring day in "the city that knows no seasons" and all seasons—the children frolicking like sea lions on the Beach, the white-faced office workers turning their eager faces to the sun from the flatness of apartment-house roofs, the cops shedding their coats and their dignity at every street corner, the whole city shrinking pleasantly together in the rare wonder of it all . . . The new busses on Market Street, snorting along in the ghostly shadows of streetcars that are no longer there—except in the memories of those who remember the madness of the street with the four-track mind; it's quieter now along the Nightmare Alley that used to frighten timid old ladies—but somehow it's no longer Market Street . . . And the white-stucco false fronts of the Western Addition houses which were mere children in the days of the fire-quake—old relics with their faces lifted, feeling young and popular again in this overcrowded era when there's a sweetheart for every hearth.

The old, bent Italians who have spent the best years of their lives shining shoes at North Beach bootblack stands—still able to smile although the Promised Land has given them not gold in the streets, but boots in their faces . . . The silent sun worshipers who crowd the benches on the tiny plateau of Union Square, comfortably parked for an hour—while in the streets all around them anxious automobiles poke their noses into the garage entrances, then draw back angrily at the implacably pleasant signs: "Sorry—Parking Space Full" . . . And wonderful, parklike Dolores Street, which bobs up and down in its own divided way from Market Street—straight into a past that had time and space for grassy parks in the middle of streets, lawns in front of houses, and sidewalks big enough for games of hopscotch under shade trees.

The picturesque firehouse on California Street, occupied by Engine Fifteen and topped off by the most magnificent weather vane in town—so definitely a part of the past that you expect a horse-drawn engine to come pounding out any moment . . . The oppressive atmosphere of Playland-at-the-Beach on a cold, wet day—the barkers standing still and silent in their overcoats, the Fun House an empty cavern of gloom, the merry-go-round playing a tinny prayer for sunshine . . . The lush green lawns of Julius Kahn Playground in the Pacific Heights sector, where the proletariat may romp in the shadow of mansions which stand coldly with their backs turned . . . And the Russ Building at five o'clock—suddenly becoming a Tower of Babble as the secretaries and stenos, so tired just an hour earlier, clatter out on their high heels like children freed from school.

The mad jumble of architecture that distinguishes Russian Hill—huge apartments and tiny back houses, formal gardens and unkempt patches of lawn, empty lots and mysteriously unfinished apartment houses . . . The garlic-flavored signs on the stores and offices along Columbus Avenue, singing their own Italian Street Song for your eyes and reminding you dreamily of faraway places you've never seen . . . Tenth and Mission, a notable Baghdadian intersection, where there is a service station on each of the four corners—plenty of free air, plenty of free water, plenty of free enterprise . . . And the Nob Hill gentlemen who walk their dogs in Huntington Park on many a midnight—their pajama bottoms peeking out from beneath their overcoats, their manner still as majestic as a floorwalker's.

The "Little Ghetto" of the Fillmore-McAllister area, rubbing narrow shoulders with "Little Osaka" and "Little Harlem"—a few thought-provoking blocks majoring in minorities . . . The massed neon signs along lower O'Farrell Street, their raucous red heightened by the driving rain, their reflections casting a weird upward glow on every strange passing face . . . The little bookshop in Old St. Mary's, always with a half-dozen volumes ranged in its small windows quite conservatively—so that you could never accuse it of advertising . . . And McDonald's fantastic secondhand book-store on Mission, a cavernous treasure trove for the bargaining literati, stacked from floor to ceiling with everything from *True Detective Tales* to *Das Kapital*—with Mr. McDonald himself, a character straight from Dickens, presiding urbanely over his cut-rate classics.

The lovely homes ranged along the bluffs of Sea Cliff, where the residents may gaze at the Golden Gate Bridge from the ocean side; an exclusive view for the exclusive few . . . The unbathed Skid Rowgues who line up for a sunbath in front of the Salvation Army on Howard Street—men with darkness in their hearts trying to get color in their cheeks . . . The never-changing downstairs lounge at the Mark, where the Same Old Faces sit in the Same Old Places and talk the talk of people with nothing to talk about except each other; the Social Register—ringing up a "No Sale" . . . And the shiny black limousines lined up for rent on Geary Street near Powell—the trappings of millionaires, available for a few dollars to those who need a King-for-a-Day-Dream.

The scores of tiny coffeeshops in the theatrical hotel sector, serving breakfast in the afternoon to pancaked girls who go to work with the sunset and to bed with the sunrise—leading upside-down lives in a world which is hardly rightside up . . . The tiny restaurant that nestles on California Street between the great stone buildings of the financial district—and is known as "Mom's Home Cooking" . . . That fantastic old theater 'way out on Mission, which was built solely

263

to put a competitor out of business; when that was accomplished, it closed . . . And the clusters of spotlights which bathe the Shell Building in gold, creating a forever-amber landmark on the skyline.

The psychopathetic ladies of the night who patrol streets like Larkin and Mission in the endless hours before dawn—speaking to passing men in a dead voice that invites no answer . . . The deadpanned old men sitting silently by the hour in the pool halls of Market Street and North Beach, watching others enjoy themselves from behind Life's eight-ball . . . The row after row of tiny, all-alike hotels along Turk, Eddy, and Ellis streets—as monotonous, as hard to identify as the men who inhabit them . . . And lower Mason Street at three in the morning—a hurly-burlycue of boisterous soldiers and sailors, double-parked cabs, dames who've had that one too many, all-night drugstores and hamburgers; just about all that's left of the town they called "Frisco!"

Grant Avenue and Post Street, the crossroads of Baghdad-by-the-Bay, where (if you stand there long enough) you can see everybody in San Francisco . . . The always freshly painted buildings of Alcatraz, glowing so brightly in the afternoon sun that for a second you forget it's inhabited by men who are deserted together on an island . . . That institution called the Bay City Grill, where the old-time waiters still follow the ancient habit, at times, of totaling your check for you right on the tablecloth . . . And the shabby gospel singers, shouting out their hearts and the glory of God at Third and Howard—while their audience lounges around on fireplugs and against telephone poles, shutting their ears and listening only with their half-closed eyes.

The frank, open windows of Telegraph Hill's miniature castles, whose occupants gape at the gapers every bit as blandly as the gapers gape at them . . . The "Portals of the Past" service station on the crest of Nob Hill, a stone's throw from the Pacific-Union Club—whose front door is also a portal of the past . . . The death of a dream in cluttered-up, run-down Sutro Heights—once the pride of a millionaire, now a sore sight for eyes that remember its beauties and turn away from its decay of today . . . And the huge neon star that revolves slowly and majestically atop the Sir Francis Drake to advertise a saloon in the sky—easily outshining the small electric cross that marks a church in the dark valley far below.

Tourists standing smellbound at Fisherman's Wharf, staring in disbelief at the huge pots of boiling water and asking the question they always ask: "You mean you *actually* throw them in *alive?*"—as the attendant, too bored to answer, nods curtly and reaches for the sacrificial crab . . . The wonderful contrast of that neat little chicken ranch under the massive approach to the Golden Gate Bridge at Fort Point—the chickens cluck-clucking around as though well satisfied that while they might not be able to build such a miracle as the span overhead, neither can a man lay an egg . . . And out-of-townies staring through open mouths at the ring of lobsters on display in the windows of Bernstein's Fish Grotto on

Powell Street—tourist-trapped by San Francisco's oldest shell game.

Chinatown's fine ladies and merchants, heading up Grant Avenue around eleven o'clock each morning for the little places that serve a tiffin of tea and steamed buns—an old Spanish custom among the Chinese . . . The shadowy waiting station of the long-dead Powell Street Railroad Company at Fulton Street and Seventh Avenue—a sentimemento of the days when the cable cars ran out to the Park instead of into the red . . . The long-ago-and-faraway atmosphere at Robert's-at-the-Beach on a Sunday night, filled with oldsters who become slightly nostalcoholic and youngsters who aren't yet aware that they're filling up with memories for future use . . . And Kearny Street in the Hall of Justice region, one part of the rundown-downtown sector that preserves some of the rough, tough color of an earlier San Francisco—as unpretty as it's unphony.

The treat of treating your eyes to true magic—at sundown, on the terrace behind the Cliff House, with the endless Beach sprawled out on your left, the Golden Gate yawning with dignity at your right, and Seal Rocks in front of you, thrillhouetted sharply against a sun sinking with amazing swiftness into the great ocean . . . Baghdad-by-the-Bay!

INDEX

267

INDEX

INDEX

INDEX

INDEX

COMSTOCK EDITIONS

Tracing its roots back to the 1969 publication of *Trask* by Don Berry, Comstock Editions has sought the finest work on the rich heritage of the American West. We believe its unique character cannot be defined by just one kind of writing, so we look for a mixture of fact and fiction. We hope this includes new works as well as classics by the great writers of the region. We are unique in presenting this collection in inexpensive, small-format editions such as this.

We welcome your suggestions for old favorites, long out of print, that you would like us to consider reprinting. We would also like to hear about your favorites in current reading about the West. Since we are a reprinter of previously published books, we cannot consider any original manuscripts. Drop us a note and indicate if you would like to be placed on our mailing list for news of future releases.

The Editors
Comstock Editions
3030 Bridgeway
Sausalito, CA 94965

You will also enjoy these other
Comstocks about San Francisco and the West . . .

ONE MAN'S SAN FRANCISCO, Herb Caen
A portrait of the City as only Herb Caen could present it. If you
have ever sent a day in San Francisco, you know that his daily
column is worth the rice of a hundred guidebooks. This collection
was prepared for the bicentennial as his gift to the City.

031-7 $3.95

SEA ROUTES TO THE GOLD FIELDS, Oscar Lewis
The story of the men who took the 18,000 mile journey to
California in 1849-1852. They risked their lives to join the race to
the gold fields and the fortune they dreamed of finding there.

044-9 $4.50

ESCAPE FROM ALCATRAZ, J. Campbell Bruce
Much more than the book behind the celebrated movie, this tells
the whole story of the rise and fall of Alcatraz as the most dreaded
of America's prisons. It is now one of the most visited landmarks
in the country.

003-1 $3.95

Special until current stocks are gone . . .

THE MADAMS OF SAN FRANCISCO, Curt Gentry 015-5 $2.95
One hundred years of the City's bawdy history

GREAT CRIMES OF SAN FRANCISCO, Dean W. Dickensheet
033-3 $2.50
True crime as fascinating as any fiction

THE HATCHET MEN, Richard H. Dillon   027-9 $2.50
The days before the earthquake when the tongs ruled Chinatown

for details about ordering these books see the next page . . .

COMSTOCK EDITIONS
A bookshelf filled with the
rich tradition of the American West

Tough Trip Through Paradise, Andrew Garcia.
An unforgettable portrait of the last days of the
frontier from the recently discovered diaries of
a man who lived among the Indians.

008-2 $3.95

Trask, Don Berry. A novel of the first encoun-
ters of the mountain men and the Indians of
the Northwest coast. A classic.   001-5 $3.95

A Majority of Scoundrels, Don Berry. The authentic story of the legendary trader-trappers of
the Rocky Mountain Fur Country and the opening of the Mountain West.   028-7 $3.95

The Big Four, Oscar Lewis. The story of the
building of the Central Pacific Railroad and the
men behind it—Stanford, Hopkins, Crocker, and
Huntington.   042-2 $4.50

The Flying North, Jean Potter. The story of
the bush pilots of Alaska based on interviews
and first-hand accounts. An amazing story of
pioneering aviation.   018-X $3.95

We hope you can find these books at your local
bookstore. If not, you can order them from us
by sending a check or money order for the price
of the book plus one dollar for the first copy
and seventy-five cents for each additional copy.
A free catalog of Comstock books is available
from this address:

Comstock Editions, Inc., Dept. 457
3030 Bridgeway Blvd.
Sausalito, CA 94965